E
99
.N3
F62
1988

Forster, Elizabeth
W.

Denizens of the
desert

DUE DATE

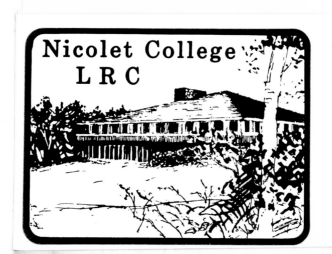

Nicolet College
L R C

Denizens of the Desert

Navaho woman, child, and lambs, 1932

Denizens of the Desert

A Tale in Word and Picture
of Life Among the Navaho Indians

Elizabeth W. Forster and Laura Gilpin

Edited and
with an introduction by
Martha A. Sandweiss

University of New Mexico Press
Albuquerque

Published in cooperation with the Historical Society of New Mexico

Library of Congress Cataloging-in-Publication Data

Forster, Elizabeth W.
  Denizens of the desert : a tale in word and picture of life among the Navaho
Indians / Elizabeth W. Forster and Laura Gilpin ; edited and with an introduction
by Martha A. Sandweiss.
         p.   cm.
  "Published in cooperation with the Historical Society of New Mexico."
  Bibliography: p.
  ISBN 0-8263-1086-9
  1. Navajo Indians—Social life and customs.
  2. Indians of North America—Southwest, New—Social life and customs.
  3. Forster, Elizabeth W.—Correspondence.
  4. Public health nurses—Navajo Indian Reservation—Correspondence.
  I. Gilpin, Laura.
  II. Sandweiss, Martha A.
  III. Title.
E99.N3F62 1988
979'.00497—dc19   88-10669

Contents

List of Illustrations

ALL PHOTOGRAPHS ARE BY LAURA GILPIN.

Frontispiece: Navaho woman, child, and lambs, 1932

Introduction

Letters

Acknowledgments

For their assistance with this book I would like to thank: Alfred Bush, curator, Princeton Collection of Western Americana, Princeton University, and Paula Stewart, Amon Carter Museum. Special thanks go to Elizabeth Forster's family, especially Jerry Richardson and Elizabeth Richardson, and to my husband, Robert Horowitz, who has also been a health care worker among the Navaho people.

—Martha A. Sandweiss

Foreword

Denizens of the Desert is a significant contribution to the continuing copublication series of the University of New Mexico Press and the Historical Society of New Mexico. Previous volumes have brought to light a variety of topics of New Mexico history that might not otherwise have been published, including memoirs, biographies, regional studies, and documentary histories. The critical approval accorded those other volumes is certain to extend to this one.

Laura Gilpin needs no introduction to the student of southwestern history. Her camera recorded some of the most important features of the area, its history, and people. Her book on the Navaho people, *The Enduring Navaho,* has become a classic photographic study. *Denizens of the Desert* combines her pictures with a series of letters written by her close friend, Elizabeth W. Forster.

Elizabeth Forster traveled with Laura Gilpin to the Navaho reservation in the fall of 1930 on a camping trip and vacation. Forster was supervisor of the Colorado Springs Visiting Nurse Association, and Gilpin, who took along her cameras to photograph archaeological sites, was a professional photographer. By chance and because of lack of gasoline, they ended up in the remote Navaho country. They befriended and were befriended by the Navaho who appeared out of the desert to help the stranded pair. Because of this incident, Forster returned in November 1931 to begin an eighteen-month residence in Red Rock as a field nurse. She provided the only medical care available in the area. This book includes the letters written during her stay in Red Rock from late 1931 until April 1933, along with photographs taken by Gilpin, some of which have never been published before. In the 1930s and 1940s the two women collaborated on editing the letters and photographs with the idea of attracting a publisher. Chance, World War II, and Forster's poor health delayed the project until it was set aside and then forgotten.

In 1979 the Gilpin papers were bequeathed to the Amon Carter Museum in Fort Worth, Texas, where the Forster letters were rediscovered. Martha Sandweiss, adjunct curator of photographs at the museum and the author of a biography of Gilpin, edited the letters and photographs for this present edition. The Historical Society of New Mexico is very proud to copublish this volume with the University of New Mexico Press.

The current officers and members of the Board of Directors of the Historical Society of New Mexico are: Spencer Wilson, president; Charles Bennett, first vice president; Michael L. Olsen, second vice president; John W. Grassham, secretary; M. M. Bloom, Jr., treasurer; and Carol Cellucci, executive director. The members of the Board are: John P. Conron, Thomas E. Chavez, Richard N. Ellis, Austin Hoover, John P. Wilson, Albert H. Schroeder, William J. Lock, Myra Ellen Jenkins, Susan Berry, Darlis Miller, Robert R. White, Robert J. Torrez, Elvis E. Fleming, Mary Jane Garcia, and David Townsend.

—Spencer Wilson

Denizens of the Desert

Elizabeth Forster, ca. 1930s

Introduction

Elizabeth Forster and Laura Gilpin came by their interest in the Navaho by chance. In the fall of 1930, they loaded an old, much-traveled Buick with camping supplies and drove southwest from Colorado Springs toward the north rim of the Grand Canyon. For Forster, it was a break from her job as supervisor of the Colorado Springs Visiting Nurse Association; for Gilpin, it was a working vacation. A professional photographer, she was eager to make the pack trip into Betatakin, to photograph the cliff dwellings for a series of lantern slides on southwestern archaeological sites. The two women visited the ruins, then drove south toward Chinle for their first view of Canyon de Chelly. But some twenty miles north of Chinle in a remote area of the Navaho reservation, they ran out of gas. After a night spent camping under a starry desert sky, Gilpin set off on foot in search of help or gasoline, and Forster remained behind to guard the car. "From what I don't quite know!" Gilpin later mused. After a two-and-one-half-hour hike of more than ten miles Gilpin reached Frazer's Trading Post, obtained some gas, and rode back to her car with the trader's wife. Gilpin later wrote to her friend, "I remember imagining how worried you must have been over my long absence. Never will I forget topping a gentle rise in the undulating desert and seeing the lonely car completely surrounded by Navaho Indians, like a swarm of bees about a honeysuckle. When we arrived there you were in the midst of the gathering, happily playing cards with your visitors!"[1] The friendly concern of the Navahos made a deep impression on them both. A year later Forster accepted a job as a public health nurse in the isolated Navaho trading settlement of Red Rock, Arizona, in the Four Corners region. Gilpin made frequent visits, taking advantage of the Navahos' high regard for her friend to make an extraordinary photographic portrait of Navaho life.

Denizens of the Desert is a collection of the letters that Forster wrote during her eighteen months in Red Rock, from November 1931 to April 1933, interspersed with Gilpin's photographs. More than fifty years ago the two women began to prepare the project for publication. But the depression and then the war dampened publishers' enthusiasm, and after the war Gilpin and Forster recognized that the enormous changes taking place on the Navaho reservation rendered these memoirs out of date. They were no longer timely journalism and not yet critical history. Gilpin set to work on a larger book about the Navaho people, eventually published in 1968 as *The Enduring Navaho*, and Forster's letters were put aside.

Now with the passing of time Forster's letters, which were rediscovered among the papers Gilpin bequeathed to the Amon Carter Museum in 1979, have acquired the value of personal history. They provide a straightforward and modest account of life in a small Navaho community in the years just before federal intervention, a world war, and a reorganized tribal government began to alter a long-established way of life.They offer a record of daily activities in Red Rock, with no pretense of being a broad overview of Navaho life or ethnography. Inevitably, they also serve as a kind of autobiography, in many regards telling us more about Forster than about the people she describes. The letters are full of enthusiasm and energy, and convey the delight she took in learning about Navaho life. They make it clear that she gained the respect and admiration of the Navaho because she had great respect and admiration for them.

Indeed, this was at the heart of her success in Red Rock: she was never presumptuous or condescending in her dealings with the Navaho. When she uses the word *primitive* in these letters, Forster intends it not as a term of approbation but as an indication of the vast differences between her world and the Navaho world. She asks, "Are we not prone to over-estimate the value of [our complicated] standards and overlook the value of their own, which, I am convinced, we are far from understanding?"[2] She never presumed an understanding of Navaho ways or even a right to understand them. And thus, she could make light of her differentness. She never minded being a source of curiosity or amusement to her Navaho neighbors who delighted in her ability to tell jokes with a perfectly straight face. And she could laugh herself at the strangeness of some of her "civilized" customs. This capacity for self-humor and her openness to new experiences allowed Forster to gain the confidence of her Navaho neighbors. She shared her medicine with the local medicine men, and they shared their medicine and some of their secrets with her. In this way, she slowly and quietly began to learn about Navaho life. Her Navaho friends gave her a name, "Asdzáá Bahozhoni," the Happy One.

Through Gilpin's photographs, Forster's small world at Red Rock becomes more vivid. It was a world poised at the edge between the old ways and the new. Horse-drawn wagons were more prevalent than automobiles. Electricity and indoor plumbing were scarce, and few Navahos, save those who had returned home from boarding schools, were proficient in English. The economy still revolved around the traditional livelihoods of sheepherding and weaving, and life was regulated by the seasons and the length of the day. Outsiders, particularly single white women, were regarded with friendly, if wary, curiosity. But the trust that Forster earned was generously extended to her friend.

Laura Gilpin made at least five trips to Red Rock to visit Forster, driving down from Colorado Springs with her 8 × 10 camera and tripod packed in the back of her car. Because she wanted to make artfully composed photographs of Navaho life that she could exhibit or use in publications, she took none of the informal snapshots a casual visitor might make as mementos. Thus, there are no photographs of Forster's house or the cluster of buildings that made up the settlement at Red Rock; almost no photographs of Forster with her friends; no pictures of the unreliable old car that she used for transportation; no photographs of Gilpin herself. But there are warm, empathetic portraits of Forster's friends; still, quiet images of the interior of the Red Rock Trading Post; and dramatic photographs of the local landscape—all giving visual expression to the sense of place we get from Forster's letters.[3]

With her large view camera and tripod, Gilpin worked slowly and deliberately, talking to her subjects to enlist their cooperation in the picture-making process. Yet her formal portraits, suffused with a soft, natural light, look unstudied. Her sitters appear comfortable and relaxed. The calm implacability with which Forster's friends accepted her is best suggested by a photograph made inside the hogan of an old man named Hardbelly. Forster is shown administering digitalis to this sick man, as his family sits peacefully on the dirt floor beside him. No one seems in the least bit aware of the obtrusive presence of Laura Gilpin, probably clad in her customary khaki trousers and broad-rimmed hat, standing at the other side of the small hogan peering under the dark cloth of her camera. She was as sensitive as Forster was to the quiet traditions and particular manners of Navaho life. She was also lucky. Years later she wrote, "Fortunately the man recovered, otherwise I would be taboo in that region forever."[4]

Edward Curtis called the Navaho the "Vanishing Race" in his popular and deliberately symbolic photograph of 1904. But for Gilpin, these same people were always the "Enduring Navaho." She liked to focus on the continuing traditions of Navaho life and the resiliency of Navaho culture in the face of incursions from modern American life. Her photographs never evidence Curtis's obsessive curiosity about anthropological detail or his devotion to a romanticized past. Gilpin regarded the Navahos as individuals, not as specimans of an exotic race, and her portraits are intimate ones of particular people, made without scientific intent or effuse romanticism.

On the day in 1930 that carelessness and happenstance introduced them to the Navaho and altered the course of their lives, Forster and Gilpin were established professionals well along in their careers. They lived with their families in Colorado Springs, Colorado, the "Little London" of the West at the foot of Pikes Peak, where wealthy convalescents and sun seekers were more prevalent than miners or ranchers. Forster was forty-four years old. Born in Georgetown, South Carolina, in 1886 to an old southern family, she was a frail woman whose fragile appearance belied her physical strength and dry wit. She had studied public health nursing at Johns Hopkins University and graduated from the nursing program at Baltimore's Union Memorial Hospital in 1912. Later that year she followed her physician brother Alexius to Colorado Springs, and in 1913 joined the Colorado Springs Visiting Nurse Association. She become supervisor of the organization in 1915, and with the exception of a one-year leave during which she worked in

Hardbelly's Hogan, 1932

the South as a Red Cross nurse, she held the supervisor's position until she left for Red Rock in 1931.[5]

Laura Gilpin was five years younger. Born in Colorado Springs in 1891, but educated first by a German governess and then at private girls' schools in the East, she combined a western independence and high-spiritedness with an unfailing gentility and sense of decorum. With money saved from raising poultry on her family ranch, she went to New York in 1916 to study photography at the Clarence White School, the nation's leading school for the study of pictorial photography, and began her career as a professional photographer. She specialized in portraiture and architectural work but was recognized in this country and abroad for her still lifes and southwestern landscapes. During a bout with the flu in 1917 she returned to Colorado Springs and was nursed back to health by a woman from the Visiting Nurse Association. She and the nurse, Elizabeth Forster, discovered that they shared a belief in hard work and an interest in art, literature, music, and the outdoors. During the long hours they spent together during Gilpin's convalescence they became devoted friends, and they remained so for more than fifty years.[6]

Forster's work at Red Rock was part of an experimental public health program sponsored by the New Mexico Association on Indian Affairs, a group organized in Santa Fe in 1922 to represent the political interests of the Pueblo Indians.[7] The group later became affiliated with the larger Eastern Association on Indian Affairs in New York, and its stated purpose was to work hand in hand with the federal government "to assist the Indian Bureau in making reforms and improvements first, by cooperating with it, and second, by the actual, positive demonstration of the worth and feasibility of a given method or procedure."[8] Early on, in addition to working with the Pueblo Indians on land disputes and crafts projects, they decided to become involved in the Indian Bureau's health-care programs. In the early 1920s, these programs centered around regional hospitals staffed with government doctors and nurses. Fieldwork was carried out by "field matrons," nonmedical personnel who, with little professional supervision, did everything from home economics education to bedside nursing. The quality of this fieldwork was inconsistent, so in 1924 the Indian Service dispatched two trained Red Cross nurses to field positions to see whether they would be more effective than the field matrons.[9]

The New Mexico Association, consistent with its policy of supporting experimental field programs that would aid Indian welfare, dispatched its

Laura Gilpin, self-portrait, ca. 1928

own nurse to work with an Indian Service doctor at the northern pueblos in 1924, and sent its first nurse to the Navaho reservation, to the community of Nava, in 1928. The Navahos' nomadic way of life presented new problems in health-care delivery, and after only a few months on the job the association's nurse left, commenting that an effective job could not be done unless the nurse could "organize as a flying unit and follow her charges and their sheep wherever she could."[10]

The challenge of developing an effective nursing program for a widely dispersed population led the association to send another registered nurse to the Navaho community of Newcomb, in western New Mexico in 1929.[11] And in 1931, encouraged by the success of this operation, the association began searching for a second nurse to send to Red Rock, Arizona, some thirty-five miles west of Shiprock in the northeastern section of the Navaho reservation.

Some form of health care had been available to the Navaho in and around Red Rock since before the First World War when Dr. Robert Bell, a medical missionary, operated a dispensary there. This dispensary developed into a Presbyterian church mission hospital staffed by a medical missionary and a small corps of helpers, with back-up care provided by the two physicians and five nurses at the Indian Service hospital in Shiprock. When the Presbyterian medical mission closed, the government assumed control of its hospital building and approached the New Mexico Association with a proposal for an experimental field outpost that would be serviced by a private field nurse working in cooperation with the Indian Service medical officials in Shiprock. The New Mexico Association agreed to support the idea, and Elizabeth Forster—on the strength of both her professional training and her camping experience— got the job.[12]

Forster's family disapproved of her move; in the depths of the Great Depression she was giving up a steady and permanent job for a position with an uncertain future and a modest salary. Indeed, she might have seemed an improbable candidate for the job. She was forty-five years old, had lived with or near her family all of her life, and had a secure position with the Visiting Nurse Association. But she was also an adventurer fascinated by the heroines of Greek mythology and the romance of southwestern history, who had a long-standing commitment to social service and an interest in the outdoors. The work in Red Rock offered a chance to break away from an increasingly tedious job to try something difficult and heroic herself.

In mid-September 1931, Forster and Gilpin made a brief scouting trip to see Red Rock and the abandoned mission hospital that would become Forster's home, and to meet the missionary, the trader, and the handful of Navahos settled in the tiny community. In late October, Forster packed a trunk with warm clothes, a radio, a game of checkers, and a much-loved copy of Willa Cather's *Death Comes for the Archbishop*—the story of a nineteenth-century French priest who came to live and work among the Spanish and Indian people of the Southwest—and left Colorado Springs. She drove first to Santa Fe for a meeting with Indian Service nurses, then spent a day at the Santa Fe Indian School Hospital observing trachoma cases. Stopping at the Indian Service hospitals along the way, she then proceded to Shiprock to meet E. R. McCray, the agency superintendent for the region, and drove on to her new home in Red Rock.

Her home was in the old mission hospital, a long, low building of adobe brick with a shaded frame porch along one side, that stood on a rise of land just north of the Red Rock Trading Post. The structure was government property, and McCray had promised the New Mexico Association on Indian Affairs that the building would be made ready for Forster's arrival. But when she arrived nothing had been done, and Forster gamely installed herself in two tiny rooms with no cook stove and only a small heating stove to warm her quarters. By late November, despite a fierce blizzard, no fuel had been delivered and nothing had been done to make her dispensary usable. Forster was administering medical care from her tiny kitchen. In early December the New Mexico Association notified McCray and Indian Service health officials in Shiprock and Washington that Forster would be withdrawn unless help was forthcoming. Coal was delivered immediately and carpenters set to work on a dispensary room, but McCray never quite forgave Forster for all the trouble she seemed to have caused.[13]

Forster embraced Navaho ways as something that were at once strange and exotic, and comforting and appropriate. As she drove into Red Rock, she noted a small frame structure "showing evidence of white man's influence" that had "a pathetic air, as though lost or lonely." This, she thought, never seemed true of Navaho hogans no matter how remote. And if the architecture somehow seemed appropriate to the culture, so too did the women's long, protective shawls, and the soothing sound of the medicine man's rattle.[14]

Forster was eager to learn from her new neighbors, in part because

Elizabeth Forster with weaver, 1932

she was curious and in part because she thought it would make them more willing to learn from her. She studied weaving with the women and watched the medicine men practice their craft. Her acceptance by the medicine men made her especially proud, and after a year in Red Rock she reported to the New Mexico Association:

> When I came here . . . I soon realized that the Navahos hereabouts expected to find me antagonistic to their religious customs and were slow to consult me about illness until the medicine man had failed to help, but gradually they are showing more confidence in my good will and often notify me that they are having a sing and invite me to attend. Sometimes I am invited to practice medicine with the medicine man, sometimes am asked to await the conclusion of the sing so as to be on hand to take the patient to the hospital. I am surprised and gratified to find my medicine men friendly and often cooperative. One of them tells me with a serious twinkle that he is glad have me attend his sings and see good medicine practiced.[15]

As her letters indicate, Forster's role in Red Rock was not limited to nursing. She coached a basketball team, assisted with funerals, dispensed personal and legal advice, organized Christmas parties, and presided over a small home that was periodically a community social center, a soup kitchen, and a food distribution point. After two months she could write, "I have no time here for loneliness." Indeed, she was so busy she was virtually never alone.[16]

Her cheerful letters to family and friends, published here, convey only some of her experiences. Her formal reports to the New Mexico Association on Indian Affairs, which became less frequent and less timely as she got absorbed in her work, discuss more of the real difficulties of her job. They recount her disputes with the Indian Service agents who failed to prepare her home for her arrival or to deliver her heating coal, her unending mechanical difficulties with her car, her disappointment at the unreliability of some of the Indian Service doctors with whom she worked, and the severity of the Red Rock weather.[17]

Most important, though, her scattered reports convey the keenest sense of just how busy she was. While her letters relate the humorous situations in which she often found herself, her long conversations with Navaho friends, and the details of the ceremonies she watched, they do not convey the full scope of her medical activities. Even the reports provide only the bare details. In December 1931, just a month after establishing herself in Red Rock, she treated 138 cases, most at scheduled clinics (replete with hot soup to entice prospective patients) held in the old mission hospital where she lived. By summer, she was too busy in Red Rock to follow the local Navaho to their mountain pastures. In June she treated 225 patients in her dispensary, made 34 visits to hogans, and drove 14 cases to the hospital in Shiprock. In July, she made six 200-mile roundtrips to check on suspected typhoid cases near Sweetwater, made weekly trips of the same distance to Aneth, and treated nearly 200 cases in Red Rock. In August, while continuing her weekly visits to Aneth and treating more than 200 patients in Red Rock, she finally managed to make two overnight camping trips into the mountains to visit several communities of summer hogans.[18]

Quickly, Forster became adept at coping with the unexpected. A routine drive with a sick patient to the Shiprock Hospital thirty-five miles away, could become a hundred-mile drive to Toadlena if the hospital in Shiprock was full. Routine clinic days could become chaotic if, as frequently happened, the doctor from Shiprock failed to show up. This "weakens Miss Forster's position with the Indians and makes them feel that all white medicine is thoroughly unreliable," the New Mexico Association's field representative complained. Moreover, Forster was then obliged to house and feed sick patients until the doctor appeared or she had time to drive them to a hospital.[19]

Forster dealt with tuberculosis, appendicitis, frostbite, flu, trachoma, childbirth, mastoid infections, goitre, and scores of other ailments that she reported dutifully to her employers and rarely, if ever, to her friends. Though her work was carried out under difficult conditions in unfamiliar surroundings, it was nonetheless not that different from what she had been doing for twenty years. What seemed more novel and more interesting to write about was news of her new Navaho friends and the unfamiliar rituals of Navaho life. The letters published here are sunnier than her perfunctory reports to her employers not because Forster was trying to maintain a brave, false front, but because she was eager to share the more unfamiliar aspects of daily life and did not want to trouble her friends with the routine details of her daily work.

In addition to deleting references to family and friends, Forster edited the letters here in only one significant respect when she later prepared them for publication. She altered many of her harsh but frank comments about her close neighbor at Red Rock, Presbyterian minister Angelo James Luck, who persisted in following Forster about in an effort to turn her nursing visits into "hogan prayer meetings." Luck had begun work in Red Rock a few months before Forster arrived, but she found him utterly unsympathetic to the Navaho way of life and completely unsuited to his calling. He was, she wrote in words deleted from her final draft of these letters, "a reformed drunkard, a reformed auto mechanic, and a reformed Roman Catholic . . . a highly nervous, irascible individual, constantly planning big things and never accomplishing adequately the small ones which present themselves." His frequent temper tantrums never fazed the Navaho, but threw his frail, tuberculous wife into hysterics. And Foster had no patience with his unwillingness to assist her during medical emergencies. She feigned not to understand the missionary's antagonism toward her. Perhaps, as her translator Timothy Kellywood suggested, it was simply that "we has more friends."[20]

Forster got along well with the only other Anglos in the Red Rock community, the trader Mr. Stolworthy and his wife, whose interests, unlike Mr. Luck's, seemed to lie with the Navaho, and she enjoyed her regular visits to their trading post, where she could catch up on all the local gossip. But her contact with other Anglos was limited—unlike many Indian Service teachers or hospital employees she did not live and work in a white enclave—and her real friends at Red Rock were drawn from the Navaho community. She received only sporadic visits from Margaret McKittrick Burge, the New Mexico Association's field representative, who more than once was prevented from reaching Red Rock by washed out roads or drifting snow. And Forster's name is conspicuously absent from the social column of the Shiprock newspaper that reported the comings and goings of other outlying workers in the surrounding Navaho communities, for Shiprock parties held little interest for her. She spent what few free days she had driving Navaho boys to a basketball game in Colorado Springs, taking a select few friends to see the collections of the Indian Arts Fund in Santa Fe, or watching yet another Navaho ceremony.

By early 1933, the major backers of the New Mexico Association on Indian Affairs were feeling the effects of the depression, and the continuation of the group's nursing programs seemed in doubt as the association fell behind on its monthly payments to its field nurses. In Red Rock the local Indian Bureau superintendent, E. R. McCray, made Forster's life even more uncertain by failing to deliver the promised winter coal supply. Then in March he appropriated her dispensary as a dining room and announced that the mission hospital building in which she had been living and working would be taken over by the government as a day school. Forster, with her adamant dislike of the boarding school system, could hardly protest.[21]

She reported these developments to her friends and associates, but kept the true source of her difficulties with McCray to herself. Their differences went deeper than squabbles over facilities and supplies. McCray agreed with the senior physician at the Shiprock Hospital, who wrote,

> It is the medicine man, averaging 1 in every 10 in the population, who with his great hold on the people is largely responsible for the pauperizing of the Navahos. For the hospital to do something to replace his influence rather than to play into his hands will strike at the fundamental evil, socially, morally, and economically, among the Navahos today.[22]

Forster, on the other hand, worked closely with the medicine men and recognized the power and importance of their role in Navaho life. She and McCray represented two diametrically opposed views as to the importance of Navaho traditionalism and disagreed fundamentally as to how outsiders could best work with the Navaho to effect any kind of change. Forster depended on the federal government and its agents for her housing and living supplies. If local officials would provide neither the moral support nor the physical amenities necessary to sustain her work, she decided it would be best to leave.

The New Mexico Association on Indian Affairs began exploring the possibility of moving Forster to Crystal, New Mexico, where the local traders, Mr. and Mrs. Charley Newcomb, had repeatedly asked for a nurse and where the local Bureau of Indian Affairs superintendent seemed more likely to support Forster's efforts. But such a switch could not be made without the approval of the proper authorities in Washington, so writer Oliver La Farge, president of the National Association on Indian Affairs, began negotiating with John Collier, the newly installed Commissioner of Indian Affairs. Collier explained that there was no reason that the association should not drop its nursing program at Red Rock if it so desired, as he understood that there "has been some lack of cooperation which has made the functioning at this place difficult." However, before he approached the superintendent of the Crystal region he wanted the association to consider carefully the implications of disrupting an established service.[23]

Elizabeth Forster and Navaho child, 1932

While these negotiations proceded between Collier and La Farge, Forster withdrew from the employ of the New Mexico Association on Indian Affairs. The situation in Red Rock had deteriorated still further. McCray had refused to give her a new dispensary despite the availability of space and was making free use of her interpreter. Moreover, Forster was broke. The association owed her more than $430 in salary and expenses. In mid-April she firmly demanded her back pay, regretting that she could not make a more quiet exit. With typical self-effacement she noted, "I have felt for some time that as the latest addition to the staff I must be an embarrassment to the Association and I hope that my withdrawal may make the situation less acute for those remaining."[24]

The association granted her indefinite leave effective April 25 and in late spring, due chiefly to continuing financial problems, the idea of sending a nurse to Crystal was abandoned. Forster never got an opportunity to return to work among the people she had come to love.[25]

Gilpin went to Red Rock to help Forster pack for her trip home. "Our departure was more than touching," Gilpin reported. "It makes me sick to think of all the work she has done at Red Rock being stopped and no one to carry it out." Forster concurred. "Need I say that I shall leave Red Rock with very genuine regret, for I feel that the Indians here are most friendly and appreciative of what we have endeavored to do for them." She added, "It was gratifying to have them voluntarily invite me to their ceremonies and sand paintings and to find the medicine men very willing to cooperate on increasingly frequent occasions."[26]

In vain, Forster's Navaho friends protested her departure. Just a few weeks after she left Red Rock, Francis Nakai, who appears as one of the principal characters in these letters, wrote to Oliver La Farge:

> . . . There is one great part which we had lost is a *Field Nurse* here at Red Rocks Arizona. We had a nurse here whom was a great friend to the Navajos. Her name was Miss Elizabeth Forster from Colorado Springs. We miss her whole lot. Some of the Navajos didnt hardly believe yet when she left Red Rocks to stay home. Miss Elizabeth Forster done all she could with her work in every way among us people whom Navajos all like her. And we just simply couldn't get along without a Nurse. There is a Gov. Field Doctor come out once a week at Red Rock for treatment. But that isnt enough for us Navajo people. We want a field nurse that could stay here. So we are asking you people Eastern Association on Indian Affairs we want Miss

Elizabeth Forster and Navaho women, 1932

Elizabeth Forster back for our Field Nurse to Red Rocks. And build a House to stay in so she will be Independent. . . .[27]

Gilpin and Forster passed through Red Rock to visit old friends on a vacation trip in 1934. After that, they did not return for sixteen years.

Forster had set relatively modest goals for herself. She wanted improved hygiene and better medical practices, and hoped that a more community-oriented education system might be established for the Navahos living on the reservation. Her most ambitious hopes were for a day school that would serve one good meal a day and a community center where older people could gather.[28] But she did not want to change the political structure or social organization of the Navaho world; she wanted to work within the framework of the culture that was there. Accordingly, her triumphs were quiet ones, as she brought improved health to the scores of Navaho people living in and around Red Rock.

The success of Forster's work and the success of similar projects carried out by other field nurses working for the New Mexico Association on Indian Affairs and the American Red Cross did have an impact on Indian Service health care policy. By the mid-1930s, nurses formerly employed by these private agencies held influential positions within the Indian Service nursing administration, and the agency had committed itself to a field nursing program. Between 1924 and 1934, the number of field nurses employed by the government grew from three to ninety-eight, while the number of field matron positions dropped from sixty-three to six. But the health care programs established in Red Rock were not carried on. By 1941, it was the untrained Indian Service teachers at the Red Rock Day School who bore the responsibility for treating children's impetigo sores and dispensing the medicine left by traveling physicians. When Forster and Gilpin made return trips to the Red Rock region in the early 1950s, they encountered many old Navaho friends who had received no medical care since Forster's departure.[29]

When Forster returned to Colorado Springs in April 1933, Gilpin encouraged her to collect the letters she had written to family and friends about her nursing experience at Red Rock, "to delete all personal matters and arrange the letters in good sequence," to prepare them as a book. Gilpin offered to contribute her photographs to the project, and by fall Forster, who was still without a full-time job, was busy editing her letters.[30]

Early in 1934, Forster joined the Emergency Recovery Administration in Park County, Colorado, and within a few months was promoted to state supervisor of the ERA's nursing program. In 1935 she and Gilpin became partners and organized the Friendfield Turkey Farm, a poultry operation located near Colorado Springs in Woodland Park and named after the old family plantation in South Carolina where Forster was born. When the ERA disbanded in 1936, Forster moved to a Woodland Park cabin overlooking Pikes Peak to assume management of the farm and an increased flock of birds. Gilpin, busy with her photographic business, helped out on the weekends and handled purchasing and marketing arrangements for the gourmet turkeys they sold to restaurants and the mail-order trade. The two women enlarged the business in 1937 and borrowed money to expand it again in 1939. Then, despite a contract with an Omaha poultry company, Gilpin and Forster lost everything; victims, they thought, of a jealous competitor and a conniving inspector who downgraded their prime turkeys.

They sold some of their Woodland Park land and split their remaining debts. Gilpin continued to pursue her photographic work, specializing in portraiture and architectural work. Forster returned to Colorado Springs and in 1940 started a guest house for vacationing sun seekers.

Through all of this, the two women maintained their interest in the Navaho book project. In 1937, Gilpin submitted the manuscript of "Happy Hogans" to an agent in New York, revealing that Forster was doing more than merely compiling old letters. "Miss Forster has already written one successful additional letter and has at least two more outlined. . . . I assure you I will keep prodding until it is accomplished."[31]

Nothing came of this, and five years later Gilpin submitted Forster's manuscript, now given the more dignified title "Denizens of the Desert," to Walter Frese of Hastings House. Frese had just published Gilpin's *The Pueblos: A Camera Chronicle* and was in the midst of producing her second photographic text, *Temples of Yucatan*. So Gilpin stressed the photographic content of the Navaho book: "from the purely photographic point of view, I know my work in this series is better than the Pueblo book. It should be . . . it is much later work." She promoted the manuscript as a companion piece to her 124-page book on the Pueblos. Several publishing houses, she said, had been "very interested but they all made the same criticism, that it was too short. As a piece of writing this is undoubtedly true. As the text for a companion book to *The Pueblos* it is exactly right." She and Forster now conceived of the book as an alliance of text and photographs, and to reflect this the retitled manuscript bore a joint byline and the subtitle "A Tale in Word and Picture of Life Among the Navaho Indians."[32]

Hastings House neither accepted nor rejected the manuscript, finally suggesting that it be shelved until after the war. Duell, Sloan and Pearce gave the same response, citing wartime paper shortages. Gilpin was becoming increasingly ambitious for the project and was not discouraged; "I do not feel my end of it is yet finished. I need several top notch landscapes, several more good portraits, some more sheep pictures, a squaw dance series, and a sand painting if I can manage it."[33]

During the war, the interests of Gilpin and Forster turned away from the Navaho project. In 1942, Gilpin accepted a job as public relations photographer for the Boeing Aircraft Company in Wichita, Kansas. She worked there until 1944, later calling it some of the most interesting and demanding work she had ever done.

Forster's life took a less fortunate turn. In 1942 she suddenly lost the lease on her Colorado Springs guest house and was forced to find a room at Cragmor Sanitorium, a local tuberculosis hospital where her brother Alexius worked as a physician and where she now resumed her nursing work. In the spring of 1944 she began to suffer from constant headaches and debilitating body pains that in August were diagnosed as acute encephalitis. For several weeks she was critically ill, then she developed a partial right-sided paralysis. In February 1945, the disease attacked her brain and she lost her lucidity. After a period of hospitalization, she was declared legally incompetent and moved to her sister Emily's home on a Nebraska farm. For several months Forster refused to talk or even acknowledge her surroundings. As she began her slow recovery she returned to Colorado Springs to live at Cragmor with her brother Alexius.[34]

Though frail and weakened by her ordeal, she resumed nursing at the sanitorium. During the 1910s and 1920s, Cragmor had been a leading tuberculosis hospital for the well-to-do under the direction of Dr. Gerald B. Webb, with Alexius Forster as resident manager. In the early 1930s, though, amidst rumors that Dr. Forster was running an illicit abortion mill and encouraging activities not conducive to the quiet of a hospital, Webb abruptly severed his connection with the institution and moved his patients to other hospitals. Cragmor's descent was rapid; from a reknowned clinical center for the wealthy it became a hospital for the indigent elderly, tubercular veterans, and Navahos. When Elizabeth

Forster worked at the institution both before and after her illness, it bore little resemblance to the distinguished medical center it once had been.[35]

Thus, she welcomed the offer that came from Laura Gilpin in the spring of 1946. With her work at Boeing over, Gilpin was ready to launch into a new project—a photographic survey of the Rio Grande from source to mouth. She had decided to make Santa Fe her headquarters for this project, and she invited Forster to join her there.

Forster moved to Santa Fe and, despite an effort to secure a public health nursing job at a nearby pueblo, she never worked again. Physically frail but mentally sharp she, along with Gilpin, began once again to think about the Navaho book. Gilpin submitted the manuscript once more to Duell, Sloan and Pearce with a new proposal.

> So much time has gone by that I have worried for fear it is too out of date. Now an idea comes to my mind that will bring it right up to the moment. You are doubtless aware of all the conditions on the reservation, etc. . . . Investigations have [revealed] deplorable conditions. Now it seems to me that Miss Forster's book as it stands could make a wonderful background concerning the Navaho and that we could make a trip now to the reservation, see conditions for ourselves, get material and new pictures, and end the book with an up to the minute note.

Gilpin also offered to write an introduction evaluating her friend's work as "she belittled her own work out there, or rather put herself so completely in the background, that her own accomplishment is too submerged."[36]

Finally, by early 1950, Gilpin abandoned the idea of publishing her friend's letters and decided to do a Navaho book herself. She was eager to chronicle the changes taking place in reservation life since the war, and to document the remaining vestiges of traditional life. But in no way did she want to minimize the importance of Forster's work to her project. "I want Betsy to get a share in this somehow, either as a collaborationist, or whatever you suggest," she wrote her publisher, "for if it hadn't been for her taking that field nursing job, I would never have gotten my early pictures. . . ." Forster shared Gilpin's enthusiasm for the reconceived book and offered to let her unpublished letters be used in whatever way might prove useful.[37]

In March 1950, Gilpin and Forster went back to Red Rock for the first time in sixteen years. "The reception Betsy got was very touching . . . ," Gilpin wrote. "Some Indians immediately began asking for medicine, or relating all their symptoms. Then we found that there has never been any medical aid in that area since Betsy left . . . ."[38]

For the next eighteen years the book that both women had imagined would take just a trip or two to complete would be the focus of their lives. Gilpin's ambitions for the book grew. She envisioned a comprehensive text that would cover Navaho history and the politics and economics of Navaho life, and close with a discussion of the Navaho ceremonialism that "holds the Tribe together."[39] She began photographing in areas far from Red Rock: the tribal offices in Window Rock, the uranium mines in the Four Corners area, the fairs in Gallup, the clinic at Many Farms.

Still, the friendships that they had made in Red Rock two decades before drew Forster and Gilpin back to Red Rock again and again, and they rarely appeared at the trading post there without a bag of clothes to be left for distribution to their friends. "Once an Indian has learned to trust a person, the bond is lasting," Gilpin wrote. During the years they were away, they had followed local news through occasional letters sent by Forster's old friend and neighbor, Francis Nakai. In 1950, they saw the Nakais again for the first time in many years. They still lived in the same small frame house, not far from the site of Forster's home and dispensary. Their oldest son had been killed in Europe in World War II and almost the only object in their sitting room was the flag that had been over the boy's coffin at the time of his burial in France. Gilpin photographed the family in front of the flag. Few other pictures could so eloquently suggest the changes that had taken place on the reservation since their last visit. Gilpin and Forster sought out the Nakai family on all of their visits, and, on occasion, Francis would act as their guide. The two women followed the family to Shiprock where Francis had gotten a government job, empathized with them as he struggled with alcoholism, and rejoiced when he beat the problem and resumed farming. On a trip in 1964 they learned that Francis had died of pneumonia the winter before, and they drove back out to Red Rock to visit his widow. "Mrs. Francis burst into tears when she saw us and it took Betsy quite a while to quiet and comfort her," Gilpin wrote. "We talked to the two daughters, giving them some fruit we had brought, and, when it was time for us to go, Mrs. Francis took my hand and put into it a beautiful hand-woven belt she had recently made. As we drove away, Betsy had them all smiling and happy."[40]

Francis Nakai and family, 1950

As they traveled, Gilpin and Forster always carried with them a loose-leaf binder of photographs to use as an introduction to the people they did not know. In the summer of 1953, they brought out the pictures to show to a group of elderly women gathered in a summer shelter not far from Red Rock. When Gilpin showed the photographs that she had made inside of Hardbelly's hogan in 1932, the women began speaking rapidly in Navaho. "I pointed to the nurse in the picture, then to Betsy standing beside me," Gilpin later wrote,

> but the eldest of the three kept shaking her head. Just then a teenage boy came to see what was happening. "My grandmother says this is not the nurse, she had dark hair." Betsy leaned over taking a lock of the old lady's hair, and said, "Tell your grandmother she did too." Recognition broke through; the old woman stood up, put her head on Betsy's shoulder and her arms around her, and wept. After a few minutes Mrs. Hardbelly raised her head, shook herself, straightened her shoulders, and returned to the present.

Gilpin did not photograph her then, but returned a day or two later after she had had a chance to dress and compose herself for a picture. Gilpin had to develop her own connections in the Navaho world outside of Red Rock; but in Red Rock the memories of Forster's work remained strong, and the two women needed no introductions.[41]

After only a few trips to the reservation in 1950 and 1951, Gilpin began to realize that her optimism about an early completion date for the book was misplaced. Her own financial straits made it difficult for her to leave Santa Fe, and Forster's uncertain health meant Gilpin often had to make her trips to the reservation alone. But from Gilpin's point of view the delays in finishing the project often worked in her favor. "It takes time to make friends," she wrote. "There are some regions where other photographers have spoiled it for me by paying very high model fees, etc. Mine come through friendship and are much more genuine as a result."[42]

Gilpin's most ambitious work, *The Enduring Navaho*, finally appeared in 1968 with photographs made over a period of thirty years. The text covered such topics as the Navaho creation myth, farming and sheepraising, weaving and painting, tribal politics and education, county fairs, and sacred ceremonies. The book drew warm praise from anthropologists, historians, and photography critics, but no acclaim meant so much to Gilpin as that she received from the Navaho people

Mrs. Hardbelly, 1953

Elizabeth Forster and Paulina Barton's sister near Red Rock, 1950

themselves. She treasured the stories she heard of people going into the Red Rock Trading Post and paying one dollar a week toward their own copy of the hardback book.[43]

Gilpin's name appeared alone as the author of the book, but many of the most compelling passages of the text were based on anecdotes drawn from Forster's letters and the first-hand accounts of their return visits to the reservation in the 1950s. Gilpin did not want to slight Forster's contribution. She dedicated the book to "Elizabeth Warham Forster, R. N." "Dear Betsy," she wrote,

> This is as much your book as mine. Not only have you shared completely in the making of it, but also you have taught me to understand the Navaho People. . . . From time to time my visits revealed the work you were doing, your understanding, your patience, your kindness, and your generosity, for you literally gave of your substance as well as your knowledge and nursing skill.

Gilpin concluded, "What fun we have had evolving this book. Your help when I was after difficult pictures, your sound criticism, and your encouragement, finally, have brought the book to completion. As a tribute to our long and happy friendship, this is your book."[44]

The book proved to be Gilpin's last and most generous gift to her companion of more than fifty years. After years of failing health, Elizabeth Forster died on New Year's Day, 1972. Almost immediately, Gilpin began work on a new photographic book about Canyon de Chelly and the handful of Navaho families living there. This project remained unfinished at the time of her death in 1979.

The Enduring Navaho goes well beyond *Denizens of the Desert* in the ambitiousness of its text and the scope of its topic. But Forster's book of letters makes an important and different sort of contribution to our understanding of American life during the 1930s. Its very specificity is its strength. Here, in these letters, is the story of a traditional Navaho community just beginning to come to terms with modern American ways. It is a modest and personal story about particular people living in a small place. Forster never presumes to report more than she experienced or to make broad assumptions based on her limited knowledge of Navaho ways. Her work certainly deserves a place among the other texts written about reservation life by schoolteachers and traders, but it deserves consideration in a broader context as well. Traditional American life became a central theme for many writers and photographers during the depression, as government programs put out-of-work artists to work documenting the American scene. Gilpin herself applied for a job with the Farm Security Administration's photographic project but was rejected because her work seemed too "pictorial" for this program designed to record American life on film.[45] The Navaho people—overlooked because they did not benefit from the FSA's economic programs—were also excluded from this massive governmental photodocument of 1930s America. Working together in an isolated section of the Southwest, Forster and Gilpin documented these forgotten people, creating a warm, personal record of life among the Navaho that complements the better known photographic texts of the decade and fills a gap in our understanding of American life during the Great Depression. Assembled here, as they once hoped it would be, *Denizens of the Desert* is their tribute to a proud people living through difficult times.

1. Laura Gilpin, *The Enduring Navaho* (Austin: University of Texas Press, 1968), v.

2. See below, p. 138–39.

3. Laura Gilpin's photographic archive is on deposit at the Amon Carter Museum, Ft. Worth, Texas.

4. Laura Gilpin (LG) to Walter Frese, January 17, 1942. Unless otherwise noted, all correspondence cited can be found in the Laura Gilpin Archives at the Amon Carter Museum.

5. Biographical information about Elizabeth Forster and her family comes chiefly from her great-nephew Gerald Richardson, interview with the author, Santa Fe, January 29, 1981; and her niece Elizabeth Richardson, interview with the author, Albuquerque, August 18, 1982, notes on deposit at the Amon Carter Museum. See also "Elizabeth Forster Dies after llness," *New Mexican,* January 3, 1972; Gerald Shorb to the author, September 28, 1982; Rudolf A. Clemen, Jr. to the author, June 14, 1983; Karen Marczynski to the author, May 9, 1983.

6. For fuller biographical information on Gilpin, see Martha A. Sandweiss, *Laura Gilpin: An Enduring Grace* (Ft. Worth: Amon Carter Museum, 1986).

7. Typescript, n.d., New Mexico Association on Indian Affairs Collection (NMAIA coll.), New Mexico State Records Center and Archives, Santa Fe.

8. "National Association on Indian Affairs, Inc." [Pamphlet; annual report?], n.d (c. 1933), American Association on Indian Affairs Collection (AAIA coll.), Box 91, Princeton University Library. The Eastern Association on Indian Affairs was founded in 1924. In 1933 it changed its name to the National Association on Indian Affairs, and in 1937, following its merger with the American Indian Defense Association, the group became the American Association on Indian Affairs. Since 1947, it has been known as the Association on American Indian Affairs.

9. "Observations on Indian Health Problems and Facilities," *Public Health Bulletin 223,* (Washington, D.C.: U.S. Treasury Department Public Health Service, 1936), 18–19.

10. Margaret McKittrick, "Nursing Situation," in "Eastern Association on Indian Affairs Annual Report, 1929," Collection of New York Public Library.

11. "Eastern Association on Indian Affairs Annual Report, 1930," Collection of New York Public Library.

12. *Farmington Times-Hustler* January 8, 1932, 3:1; "Report of the Nursing Committee, New Mexico Association on Indian Affairs, 1932," NMAIA coll.; "Annual Report, 1927 (Northern Navaho Agency)," 2–4; "Annual Report, 1931 (Northern Navaho Agency)," 1–3; "Annual Statistical Report for 1932 (Northern Navaho Agency)," 2–3. These annual reports are found in "Annual Statistical Report in Superintendents' Annual Narrative and Statistical Reports from Field Jurisdictions of the Bureau of Indian Affairs, 1907–1938," National Archives microcopy #1011, roll 93.

13. "Report of the Nursing Committee, New Mexico Association on Indian Affairs, 1932," NMAIA coll.

14. See below, p. 41.

15. (Elizabeth Forster [EF] to Mrs. [Margaret McKittrick] Burge, November 7, 1932, Tsenostee project file, Box 5, AAIA coll.)

16. See below, p. 58.

17. Scattered reports can be found in the papers of the American Association on Indian Affairs at the Princeton University Library and the New Mexico Association on Indian Affairs Collection at the New Mexico State Records Center and Archives.

18. EF to Miss McKittrick, January 10, 1932, NMAIA coll.; EF to Mrs. [Margaret McKittrick] Burge, November 7, 1932, AAIA coll.

19. Margaret McKittrick Burge, "Field Trip, November 13–November 15, 1932," AAIA coll.

20. Biographical information on Angelo James Luck (1888–c.1950) courtesy of Gerald Gillette, research historian, Presbyterian Historical Society, Philadelphia. The original drafts of Forster's letters which include the references to Luck are in the collection of the Amon Carter Museum.

21. "New Mexico Association on Indian Affairs [Minutes, March 14, 1933]," AAIA coll.; EF to Mrs. Moris Burge [n.d. April 1933], AAIA coll.

22. "Annual Statistical Report for 1932 [Northern Navaho Agency]," 3.

23. See the following letters in the AAIA coll.: Margaret McKittrick Burge to Oliver La Farge, March 15, 1933; John Gaw Meem to Oliver La Farge, April 3, 1933; Oliver La Farge to Miss A. E. White, April 19, 1933; Oliver La Farge to John Collier, April 24, 1933; John Collier to Oliver La Farge, May 24, 1933.

24. EF to Mrs. Moris Burge [n.d. April 1933], AAIA coll.

25. "Bills due May 15th 1933, New Mexico Association on Indian Affairs," AAIA coll.

26. LG to Oliver [La Farge], July 10, 1933, AAIA coll.; EF to Mrs. Moris Burge [n.d. April 1933], AAIA coll.; EF, "Nurse's Report, May 1933," AAIA coll.

27. Francis Nakai to Oliver La Farge, June 18, 1933, AAIA coll.

28. EF to Mrs. Burge, January 1, 1933, NMAIA coll.; "Annual Report 1932, Mew Mexico Association on Indian Affairs," NMAIA coll.

29. "Observations on Indian Health Problems and Facilities," 19; Ruth E. Werner, *Novice in Navajoland* (Scottsdale: Southwest Book Service, 1972), 28; Ruth M. Raup, *The Indian Health Program from 1800–1955* (Washington, D.C.: Public Health Service, U.S. Department of Health, Education, and Welfare, 1959); LG to Walter Goodwin and Charles Pearce, March 28, 1950. For information on one nurse who began as a Red Cross field worker and eventually directed the Indian Service nursing programs see: Elinor D. Gregg, *The Indians and the Nurse* (Norman: University of Oklahoma Press, 1965).

30. LG to Sam Sloan, April 20, 1944.

31. LG to A. M. Sukennikoff, April 26, 1937.

32. LG to Walter Frese, January 17, 1942.

33. Walter Frese to LG, May 22, 1942; Sam Sloan to LG, April 7, 1944; LG to Sam Sloan, April 20, 1944.

34. Paul A. Draper, M.D., to J. Donald Hanley, March 16, 1945; Sandweiss, *Laura Gilpin: An Enduring Grace,* 74–77.

35. See: Douglas McKay, *Asylum of the Gilded Pill: The Story of Cragmor Sanitorium* (Denver: State Historical Society of Colorado, 1983).

36. EF to E.T. Hagburg, n.d. 1948; LG to [Walter Goodwin?] at Duell, Sloan and Pearce, n.d. [c. November 1947].

37. LG to Walter Goodwin and Charles A. Pearce, March 28, 1950; LG to Walter Goodwin, March 11, 1950.

38. LG to Walter Goodwin and Charles A. Pearce, March 28, 1950.

39. LG to Frank Wardlaw, June 17, 1967.

40. Gilpin, *The Enduring Navaho,* 248; Mrs. Edith Kennedy, interview with the author, Red Rock, Arizona, September, 1981.

41. Gilpin, *The Enduring Navaho,* 32.

42. LG to Charles A. Pearce, October 14, 1951.

43. LG to Philip Jones, November 11, 1975.

44. Gilpin, *The Enduring Navaho,* v.

45. Sandweiss, *Laura Gilpin: An Enduring Grace,* 71.

Prologue

In 1921 Elizabeth Forster and I took our first camping trip into the Southwest. We packed our tent, our sleeping bags, grub box, dog, and my heavy camera equipment into our Model T and fared forth into the unknown. We went for rest and recreation, in search of new pictures, and for the fun of exploring new country. We camped because we love it and because we believe it to be the only way really to know the great out-doors, to know the beauty of the dawn and the wonder of the night sky.

In those days it was more of an adventure than it is now. The roads were bad and filling stations few and far between. If one got into trouble it was necessary to get out again by one's own initiative, or to stay in. In all our early years of camping trips, we had many experiences, some exciting, some amusing, only one was serious, all were fun. The final result of the serious mishap is this book. It was the year when we made our first trip into the Navaho Reservation where we had gone so that I might add certain pictures to my archaeological series, and our ignorance of the country and its inhabitants led me to embark on a long hike across the desert after gasoline. This was a foolish venture, for I know now that a stalled automobile is an instant source of curiosity to any Navaho who will walk or ride miles to see what the trouble is. Had I waited as I should have done, all that followed might never have happened and we would be without a rich and interesting chapter in our lives. When we finally ran out of gasoline it seemed that we could see a hundred miles in every direction and that there was neither habitation nor human being visible. On that long, dusty, hot trek, I lived through all the tales I had ever read or heard of being lost on the desert for I knew not whether I had ten, twenty or how many miles to walk to reach water, shade, and above all a supply of gasoline. From this experience however, grew an interest in these Desert Dwellers and a deep love for the desert.

A year later, this intrepid friend of mine felt the urge to return to the reservation as a field nurse. Her tale of her life among the Navahos and her experiences as she recorded them bit by bit in her letters to her family and friends have been gathered together and are the theme of this book. During the two years she spent at Red Rock, I made several trips to visit her. It is needless to say that it was only the remarkable place she made for herself in the lives of the Indians in this region that made it possible for me to make most of the pictures in this series. I was accepted as her friend and because of their trust in her (and hers in them), I was given many rare opportunities. I could add much to this story in telling of her work as I saw it during those visits. How the Indians found that they could always depend on her, how she mysteriously understood them in spite of a language barrier, her remarkable psychological understanding of them, her unerring judgment, her willingness to undergo real hardship to carry out her work and above all the feeling the Indians had for her. This was most evident on our several return visits since she left her position there, for the way the news spread that she was in the vicinity and the way they came to see her and bring her their touching offerings, was moving to witness. But before we come to her adventures, perhaps it would be of interest to recount the history in brief of the Navahos as a tribe that you may have a better insight into the present day life of one particular region.[1]

—Laura Gilpin

1. Gilpin never wrote the historical overview with which she intended to introduce Forster's letters. However, she kept the idea in mind. Thirty years later she introduced her own book, *The Enduring Navaho* (1968), with an historical account of the Navaho people.

Letters

Colorado Springs, Colorado
September 9, 1931

Dear Emily:[2]

   Perhaps you will remember an adventure Laura and I had a year or so ago when we were lost on the Navaho desert? We wandered many miles on several roads trying to follow perplexing directions given by a trader at Kayenta, and it remained for a nice old Navaho Indian who could not speak a word of English to put us on the right road with sign directions which were perfectly clear and easily followed. Our aimless wandering, however, had consumed time and gasoline and we camped for the night on the desert, many miles from any white settlement and with no sign of human habitation anywhere visible until, with the dark, there came to us the gleam and flicker of distant Navaho camp fires. Snugly tucked in our blankets we indulged our imaginations for awhile by fancying these were signal fires informing denizens of the desert that two lone females were lost in their midst, and experienced a few nervous qualms as to our safety and comfort. By and by, as nothing happened to justify the least uneasiness, we turned to contemplation of a canopy of midnight sky thickly studded with glorious stars, and so, soothed by a marvelous sense of peace and protection which I have since associated with desert life, we fell asleep.

   Next day we set forward hopefully and travelled an encouraging distance before our gasoline was exhausted. Laura's ten mile trek through merciless sunshine and hot sand to the nearest Trading Post has become an amusing story, but it was far from funny at the time. I, meanwhile, remained on guard in the car, praying that some other wayfarer might pass that way and either let me have a little gas or overtake Laura and give her a lift. Such hope proved vain, but Laura was hardly out of sight before Navahos began to appear, afoot and on horseback, singly and in pairs, until I was surrounded by a curious inquisitive crowd. Lacking a common language we yet managed a deal of conversation and I was able to convey the information that, contrary to their evident suspicions, my trouble was not flat tires, not a broken-down car, but the lack of gasoline, and that a companion was off on foot in an effort to supply the lack. After

---

   2. Emily Forster Stewart, the fourth of the six Forster children, was born in 1888, two years after her sister Elizabeth. During the early 1930s, she lived with her husband and daughter on a Nebraska farm.

a time appeared what is known on the Reservation as a "returned student." This individual, with a mouth full of gold teeth and a gift of gab, which he was able to indulge with a fair supply of English, attached himself to my retinue as interpreter and friend. He supplied me with information about the country thereabout, the probable length of Laura's tramp, bits of local gossip concerning friends whom he found with me, and finally taught me to gamble Navaho fashion. So time passed and I was amazed at its lapse when, after four and a half hours, Laura appeared in a Trader's car with the necessary gasoline, and my desert reception was ended. From it, however, dated an interest in the Navaho which has resulted in my considering a position as Field Nurse offered by the National Association on Indian Affairs.

Laura and I are off on a scouting expedition next week to look over location, living quarters, working associates, etc., and then I shall have to decide whether or not I am willing to exchange the comfort and security of my present life of more or less ordered routine for a pioneering venture in Public Health Nursing amongst a strange people, which will present new and perplexing problems in health and psychology.

Dear Emily;

Well, I am back from my scouting expedition, and I am burning
bridges as fast as I can lest my courage fail and I settle more deeply in
the rut of civilization and let slip the chance to hitch my wagon to the
star of adventure. The lure of the star light is strong yet my inclination
wavers somewhat when I contemplate leaving a job which promises
certainty in these uncertain times, for one which is surely experimental,
and of course the breaking of the ties of friendship and daily association
grows harder while my determination strengthens.

Our voyage of exploration took us to Red Rock by way of Shiprock, to
the New Mexico–Arizona line near the only place in the United States
where four states meet at a corner. Through the tiny town of Shiprock,
built around an Indian School, along the highway we travelled to a
turnoff road which took us over a barren stretch of desert towards a
vaguely seen line of mountains some thirty miles away. From half that
distance Shiprock itself, (from which the little town has taken its name),
seemed to sail on a sea of desert, and from its stem and from its stern
extended a wall of rock which is hard to believe not man made,—but
such is often the wonder of natural things. You are, no doubt, familiar
with Laura's lovely picture of this great rock. It will, hereafter, be for me
the halfway mark to civilization, since it lies midway between my abode
and the nearest post office. The passage through the wall of stone already
seems the gateway to my home.

From Shiprock on, the road rises from the desert's arid floor and the
still distant mountains seem to profer seductive sanctuary from the
desert's heat. With this inviting vista absorbing our interest it was with a
slight shock that after descending an arroyo, crossing a wash and
climbing the other bank we came upon an infinitesimal settlement. And
this is Red Rock—the name, of course, suggested by some lovely
formations seen in the distance. The community consists of little more
than a Mission (partly abandoned) and a Trading Post. Mission property is
under a God Bless Us sign done in Navaho and the English alphabet for
all who pass to read. I wonder who can? The driveway (nothing more
pretentious than car tracks) climbs a slope between two rows of dwarfed
and dying treelets. On the brow of the hill stands the abandoned hospital
building, a small Church with bell and steeple, the Missionary's little

Shiprock from the west, 1932

house and his Interpreter's smaller one. From the Hospital porch one's attention is attracted by a lovely spreading cottonwood in whose shelter lies the long, low rock and adobe Trading Post. One other building completes the tiny settlement—a small frame structure showing evidence of white man's influence. On the desert, across the wash, it has a pathetic air, as though lost and lonely. This somehow never seems true of the native hogans no matter how remote.

Although I can claim no architectural beauty for the home I am to have in the hospital building, it is at least surrounded by beauty—beauty of a type which is new and strange to me. On three sides boundless stretches of red sand and to the west the mountains. Unbelievably varied and constantly changing color and lovely grouping of form are afforded by the sandstone cliffs which extend to the north and west, prefacing our approach to the mountains. To the southwest the mountains are nearer and the road winds up and over, through a pine and aspen forest, to Lukachukai and beyond. Throughout the desert landscape, between the mountains and the highway thirty miles to the east, there is, to the casual eye, no sign of human dwelling until one notices here and there a small structure resembling in shape an Esquimo igloo. It is built of logs covered with desert soil, which makes it practically invisible from a distance. This is a Navaho house—or hogan it is called. Its interior, of course, resembles the inside of an inverted bowl, with an opening in the center of the top to admit light and to serve as a smoke vent for the fire which is built directly below. It contains no furniture except sometimes a rudely constructed stove made from an old galvanized tub, bucket or whatnot. A stove pipe made from old pieces of tin is sometimes seen too, but the general rule is an open fire on the ground and no pipe. A coffee pot and a few cooking utensils usually hang on the log sides or are stored in a wooden grocery box. Beds consist of sheep or goat skins and a few blankets spread on the dirt floor at night and rolled against the wall in the day time. The entrance is always to the east and an old blanket generally serves as door. The passing of a car is provocation for the appearance of several Navaho dogs which give vociferous chase, and occasionally for the appearance of a picturesque native figure or two. Occasionally, too, one glimpses in the distance small herds of sheep and a few scattered cattle and horses and wonders that they are able to subsist on the scant pasture offered by desert soil.

You will be interested, I think, in an adventure we incorporated in our trip of investigation. Hearing that Earl Morris, an archaeologist friend of

Hogan in Red Rock Cove, 1932

Laura's, was excavating in the lovely red cliffs which I have mentioned, we couldn't resist the temptation to take our camping equipment and trail him in the wilds.[3] So into pre-cliff-dweller country we went and found an interesting archaeological camp of delightful personnel conveniently located for access to a number of ruins. Once within these caves, surrounded by relics of a forgotten past, things of today faded from immediate consciousness and imagination played irresistably with a long dead, primitive civilization. I cannot tell you how completely one loses one's sense of familiar identity and becomes imbued with the romance of ancient life which is suggested on every hand.

Back on our way to Santa Fe for an interview with the Association's Field Executive, we were once again tempted into sidetracking for a visit to Pueblo Bonito in Chaco Canyon. This amazing remnant of a much later and more highly developed civilization than that evidenced in our red rock cliffs of the day before, prepared us for a still later development in the Pueblos through which we passed to reach Santa Fe.

Thence we stepped back into a familiar world, and in spite of anxious qualms on Laura's part I am preparing to store my Lares and Penates and set forth on the tail of my star.

3. Earl Morris (1889–1956) directed archaeological investigations in the Southwest for the Carnegie Institute.

Santa Fe, New Mexico
November 1, 1931

Dear Laura:[4]

An uneventful trip to Santa Fe, stopping for a glimpse of Taos which Helen had never seen.[5] We got in to Santa Fe in good time last night after a very comfortable trip. My new "Chevvy" drives easily with never a groan for its heavy load.

The day has been spent in meetings with members of the Indian Association gathering what information I might as to customary procedures in my work, contacts I should make, etc. I am to work with the doctors of the Shiprock Hospital (there are two) and hospitalization is there available for cases in my district as they occur.

Tomorrow we move on stopping en route to visit Indian Hospitals at Albuquerque, Laguna and Shiprock and to see the Superintendent of the Shiprock Agency. Helen's generous insistence in coming along to help me "settle" in is the greatest comfort. Her presence lends courage to my ignorance and pleasure to my days. The country through which we travel is lovely in the golden garb of Fall and the weather has surely never been more pleasant—happy omens for life in the Southwest!

4. Laura Gilpin.
5. Helen Eyre, a friend of Forster's from Colorado Springs, accompanied her on her drive.

Red Rock
November 7, 1931

Dear Laura:

Each day I've meant surely to get a letter off to you, but the days as they have developed have not been half long enough for the accomplishment of things I have meant to do. You can imagine the discomfort in which I am living when I tell you that when we arrived Wednesday as scheduled, we found that (contrary to information I had received) nothing had been done to prepare my rooms for occupancy. No doubt you will remember how dusty and unattractive they were when we were here more than a month ago and surmise that the lapse of time has not improved their condition.

On Thursday Helen and I drove sixty-five miles to Farmington to purchase cleaning supplies and food, stopping on the way to see the Agent and secure a promise of carpenter and painter and necessary furniture as speedily as may be.

Meanwhile we are sleeping in one of the rooms at the other end of the hospital building from my quarters. It is used by the Missionary for transient guests and provides two beds and a bureau. A fortunate supply of bedding with dishes and utensils with which I had loaded the Chevvy have made living possible. Of course I am contrite for having brought Helen into such discomfort but she is a valiant sport and insists she is enjoying it! We are trying to cook on a miserable little wood heating stove which smokes with such steady determination that it takes hearty appetites to induce us to prepare our meals. Our time has been largely spent plying broom and scrub brush and we feel that my rooms are at least clean and ready for furniture when it comes.

The neighborhood is teeming with talk of a Yeibichai dance which is in progress some eight or ten miles distant and we have watched picturesque groups of gaily dressed Navahos pass on horseback and in wagons until curiosity and interest would no longer be denied and yesterday afternoon we joined the procession. Following wagon tracks in the direction you and I took to the Morris camp when we were here in September we bumped along in a cloud of dust until we found ourselves on the edge of a great throng on blanketed and long skirted figures. Perhaps you know that Navaho dances or chants, as they are generally called, are triune in character, uniting religious, medical and social festivities, presenting a beautiful and interesting spectacle. The Yeibichai,

Navaho covered wagon, 1934

sometimes called the Night Chant, is, I believe, continuous through nine days and nights. It is a very popular occasion with the Navaho and many have come great distances to attend this one, which, I am told, is being staged by two neighbors who divide expenses and share benefits.

Parking our car on the outskirts we joined the throng. There seemed several centers of interest, and choosing one conforming to prevailing custom, we squatted on the ground, part of a huge circle surrounding a group of young Navaho for whom a ceremony was being conducted by an old Medicine Man or Shaman, accompanied by two oddly masked and costumed figures representing Yei or Gods. I am too ignorant of the significance of Navaho ritual to try to describe it but I am told that this is a ceremony of initiation which must be undergone four times (once at four different Yeibichai Dances) by young candidates before they are permitted to take part in ceremonial dances.

The girl candidates wore the usual long, full Navaho skirt and draped their torsos with modesty and long, shining black hair. The boys wore breech clouts. The demeanor of audience and participants was alike in serious intentness so that we were immediately aware that this was a religious phase of the ceremony.

Next we wandered to another group and found ourselves before rudely constructed counters where food was evidently for sale or barter. Unattracted, we walked on until we approached a very large and new looking hogan. Here we were surprised to find a Park Ranger from Mesa Verde whom I had met before and he was kind enough to introduce us to a Navaho friend, who, for a monetary consideration procured for us admission to the ceremonial hogan. We were just in time to see the completion of a large and very beautiful sand painting which had been all day in the making and which must be obliterated with the setting of the sun. We were told that it was the last and loveliest of the four paintings made at this dance, each taking a day to make and being erased at sunset the same day. On entering the hogan we were instructed to turn to the left and travel clock-wise very close to the wall to avoid marring the edge of the sandpainting which covered almost the entire floor of the hogan. This we found difficult to do without stepping in the laps of the seated Navaho who circled the painting. We managed the circuit without disaster, however, and emerged with a stimulated appreciation of Indian Art. It may be superfluous to tell you that a sand painting is the depiction of sacred tradition which the Navaho is reluctant to interpret to the white man. The picture is made with colored sands which must be obtained from great distances. Gray and black are made by mixing white sand with charcoal, blue, yellow, red and white are natural sands. We were amazed by the beauty and sureness of the design and marvelled at its execution in this very difficult medium. The design is carried in the head of the Shaman who instructs assistants in its execution. The hogan floor is covered with a neutral colored sand and prepared for the picture by stroking with long sticks until it shows a lovely, even, velvet smoothness. Upon this background the colored sands are trickled from between the thumb and forefinger in the design indicated. A mistake in design is not remedied by removal of the colored sand used but is obliterated by a trickle of that used for the background.

The completed picture is truly a masterpiece of design, executed with delicate precision and beautifully subtle in color.

Helen and I are tremendously interested in every detail and are gleaning information wherever possible, and trust it is at least fairly accurate. Tonight we go to witness the final dance, which continues through the night, closing the Yeibichai at dawn tomorrow. Then Helen feels that she must start for home and I cannot urge her to stay—true hospitality bids me speed this parting guest; so I am to drive her to Gallup tomorrow to take train or bus.

Red Rock
November 9, 1931

Dear Laura:

Please don't think that I mean to continue to deluge you with letters at the present rate, but having begun to tell you about the Yeibichai I want to finish while it is fresh in my mind. Such experiences are bewildering in their strangeness and I fear time will further blur their impression.

We set forth Saturday evening armed with thermos bottles of hot coffee and several blankets, for an all night rendezvous at the Yeibichai. When we arrived at the scene of activities we found it had, with the dark, taken on an added air of strangeness and mystery. This was further enhanced by the light from many blazing fires and the dense, brooding cloud of smoke which hovered over all. As the night wore on the smoke increased in density and our unaccustomed eyes and lungs suffered so severely that we were occasionally obliged to seek refuge in my car parked at a distance with windows closed.

This time we found the crowd gathered in long lines on two sides of a space reserved for the dancers. At one end was the ceremonial hogan, before which the two patients were seated, each holding a flat basket of ceremonial meal. The other end was kept clear for the entrance and exit of the dancers, who seemed to be gathered in a sort of temporary hogan made of cedar branches, which evidently served as dressing room. Presently a group of dancers appeared and approached the patients, who sprinkled each of them with the sacred meal from their baskets. The dancers were in costumes consisting of odd masks, ornate loin cloths topped by handsome silver belts from which fox skins hung in the back like tails. They had circlets on wrists and calves from which feathers dangled, and each carried a gourd rattle in one hand and a bunch of evergreen in the other. A long prayer or chant was sung by the Shaman followed by both patients, after which the dance was begun. In this "figure" were five dancers, the Talking God and four Dancing Gods, and their song and dance was accompanied by the constant use of the gourd rattles. I wish I could give you an adequate picture of the scene—the "stage" illumined by the rosy light of many fires, the painted bodies and strange costumes of the dancers, their weird rhythmic and unmelodic song, the audience a dark mysterious mass on either side with here and there a dusky face and pair of gleaming eyes looking out from a close wrapped blanket and caught by the light from a leaping flame.

The next dance was done by competing teams of fourteen dancers each (the Talking God, twelve Dancing Gods and a Clown), one team following another throughout the night. The Navaho were evidently much interested in the performance and respective merits of the several teams, but it grew monotonous to us and we were glad on several occasions to slip away to the car for refreshment and relief from the smoke. We were there sufficiently withdrawn from our absorption in the amazing spectacle to laugh together at the consternation some of our friends would doubtless feel if they suspected our "whereabouts." But never for an instance were we made to feel uncomfortable by the strangers whose celebration we had invaded uninvited. Their attitude toward us was invariably grave, dignified and courteous.

The dance broke up at dawn with the singing of the Bluebird Chant and we hurried home for a few hours sleep before starting our one hundred and twenty mile drive to Gallup.

The lovely, warm, perfect fall weather which met us has lasted through Helen's visit, but yesterday it clouded and I drove home from Gallup alone in a dismal rain. The road from the highway in seemed interminable with landmarks wiped out by the dark, and I was convinced that I was on the wrong road and hopelessly lost on the desert again, but at length I came to the precipitous curves semicircling Little Shiprock hill and was reassured—though the curves were frighteningly skiddy in the rain. Today has been partly rainy, partly cloudy, but just now the setting sun has emerged from the clouds and a sky of the loveliest colors seems to promise good weather tomorrow. The world from my window is lovely and fresh after its bath.

Red Rock
November 15, 1931

Dear Helen:

It rains and rains—has done so almost constantly since you left, and the road out is unfit for travel. It is surprising how dismal our world has become. You would not recognize it for the brilliant landscape you explored with me ten days ago. Not a mountain is visible, and a dense gray veil of cloud obscures the lovely color which glowed so vividly in the mid-day light, paled enchantingly to pastel tints at sunset and returned in gradually increasing beauty with the dawn. Thanks to the Yeibichai we saw the sun around and I know the beauty that is hidden by the clouds!

Monday I was cheered by the appearance of a truck from the Agency. It brought some Montgomery Ward furniture for me, a brown iron bed, a small bedside table, two chairs and a bureau. No stove, so I continue to shiver all day and hurry into bed at night thanking heaven for the ample supply of good warm blankets something prompted me to bring with me. I am beginning to grow anxious about my trunk and radio, of which I have had no word, and it seems ages since I have had news from the outside world.

The Missionary still insists that I attend morning prayers daily with his family and if I am delayed he brings them to me.[6] Patients are coming to see me in increasing numbers for treatment of minor ailments and are beginning to send for me to come to their hogans when they are too sick to come to my dispensary. To my consternation the Missionary finds this an opportunity to spread the Gospel and accompanies me with Bible and hymn book, and my nursing visit becomes a hogan prayer meeting. I listen as he "tells the story" and find it bewildering even without the complication of interpretation and am sure that by the time Grant, the Missionary's interpreter, has rendered his version it must be entirely incomprehensible to the Navaho. Apparently knowing nothing of the faith they seek to destroy, some of these determined Mission workers term it devil worship and superstition, and yet fail utterly to present Christianity in a form which primitive minds might grasp.

6. For information on the missionary, Angelo James Luck, see above, p. 12–13.

Red Rock
December 3, 1931

Dear Emily:

Here I have been installed in my new home for several weeks with scant opportunity for letter writing. I am still camping, more or less, as the Agency is slow in getting conveniences to me. After my first few days here when the weather was sunny and warm it turned cold and began to rain, and it has been raining, snowing and growing colder ever since. Just now the weather is bitter but I am snug and warm indoors with a good kitchen range and a supply of wood and coal received just before the thermometer touched bottom. It is still impossible to settle permanently in my rooms as I am daily expecting carpenter and painter, but my stove and radio keep me comfortable and happy. Meanwhile I have written for rugs, curtains, bookshelves, a small table or two and a chest of drawers from home, as hope of securing adequate furnishing from the Agency diminishes. Am also having a box couch made which will accommodate the storing of extra blankets, linen, etc., and provide a bed for guests.

You asked about my neighbors. The Trader family is very nice and friendly, though I have seen little of them as the Trader has been busy buying and selling sheep through the past month.[7] After several weeks of sheep buying from the Navaho he has to herd and drive the animals sixty-five miles to Farmington to be shipped. This takes more than a week and food and water have to be transported with them. His family (his wife and three small children) are visiting relatives while he is thus engaged, and a nephew is keeping the store for him. Of the Missionary and his family, Helen tells me she has written you. The Missionary's interpreter, Grant, is an agreeable, accommodating young Navaho who has a fairly good sized opinion of his own ability and importance. His wife, Lillie, is bafflingly Navaho and their two-year-old Grace is an amusingly interesting and independent little individual whose personality is placid.

My only other English speaking neighbor is Francis Nakai, who lives in the little frame house across the wash. He has a perfectly charming and very friendly wife who has never been "from home" and who speaks no English. Her long black hair, always shining as though freshly washed, is drawn into an hourglass bunch in the back, securely tied with strands

7. The Stolworthy family.

Mrs. Francis and corn, 1933

and strands of white wool. Her very full and ruffled skirt of yellow cambric is reversible and is trimmed on one side with bright red bands and on the other with rows of black serpentine braid. A blouse of a rather vivid dark blue is trimmed with quantities of silver buttons about the collar and down the opening, and around her neck hang strands of coral, wampum, and turquoise. A dozen or more ten cent pieces trim each sleeve. Brown buckskin moccasins, silver button trimmed, and a gay shawl complete her costume. The shawl is worn over the head out of doors and dropped to the shoulders indoors.

The Ute woman is another charming individual who lives nearby. Rumor hath it that she was stolen when quite small from the Utes and has grown up with the Navaho. She is said to have had five husbands and I can easily credit the story. At sixty, or thereabout, she retains a spontaneity and vividness of personality which has its effect on all her "contacts" whether we are able to converse intelligibly or not. Indeed a common language seems of little importance to her and she manages miraculously to make her meaning clear, especially if she is out of coffee or "sugie" and wishes a neighborly hand-out. Unlike Mrs. Francis, she is untidy in appearance and far from clean, so that I marvel at myself when I welcome her cordially to a meal. Though I know she is unaccustomed to the appointments of my simple table I would not guess it from her manner. She simply "follows suit" with dignity and decorum and we enjoy many a dish of gossip with our tea. How she makes her stories clear, how I manage to extract their meaning, I cannot tell you, but 'tis done.

In order that you may not jump to the conclusion (which this letter suggests) that my days are spent hugging the fire and gossiping with my neighbors, I enclose a few extracts from my daily record.

Man—(trachoma) eyes treated.

Baby—with diarrhea, diet and treatment outlined to mother.

Ute Woman—aspirin for headache, cathartic—too much Yeibichai.

Woman—ear irrigated to remove louse. Abdominal tumor discovered.

Man—complaining of pain in chest. Suspected nothing serious. Found he really wanted to sell me some mutton!

Child—extensive impetigo on face. Allowed the removal of scabs and the application of ointment without a murmur.

Ben Lee's baby to hospital. Pneumonia—died later.

The Ute woman, 1934

Hogan visited—Old man (Yellow Mexican). Chill last night, pain in chest, general aching, headache, temperature 101. Refuses to be taken to hospital. Visited hogan next day. Yellow Mexican not at home—out herding sheep in the rain! Rumor later reported his complete recovery.

Man—ammoniated merc. ointment for three children with impetigo.

Woman—with badly abcessed gums. Local treatment. To go to Hospital for treatment.

Man—"toothache medicine" (oil of cloves) for wife.

Yellow Horses—scabies. Sulpher ointment.

Treatment and diet outlined for two babies with diarrhea.

Child—treated for impetigo.

Bitter Water's mother—cough syrup.

John Red House's wife—liniment.

It seems strange to have no names for my patients. The best I can do is to use those given or interpreted by white men. These seem most often inspired by distinguishing marks of feature or dress. Here are some:

John Redhouse
Yellow Mexican
Red Mexican
Hardbelly
Jim Ferryboat
Navaho Jim
Big Nose
Bushy Head
Hosteen Nez
Hosteen Begay
Killed a Mexican, and my favorite, Killed a White Man
Sometime a name with Spanish flavor, as Mercedes
Too many Red Blouses and Green Blouses or Shirts
Blue Skirts and Yellow Skirts
Jewelry is also used in designation.

The trips to hogans and hospital are difficult and take an unbelievable amount of time owing to the condition of the roads. The snow is deep and badly drifted in places so that roads are obliterated, and we get stuck and must dig the car out with exasperating frequency. My need for an interpreter is urgent and I am making every effort to secure one. Difficulties present themselves—notably living quarters.

Red Rock
December 30, 1931

Dear Marion:[8]

Considering your comfort I have been glad many times that you could not accept my invitation to come a-pioneering with me, though at last I am comfortably if not luxuriously settled in my two and a half rooms. Contrary to expectations I am not to have a bath room, so the end of the hall which was to have been used for that purpose has been converted into a tiny bedroom large enough only to hold bed and lamp stand, a bureau and small wash stand, a window at one end, the other curtained for a clothes closet. This leaves my large room for a living room, and it is very comfortable with furnishings from home—familiar belongings which make me at once more comfortable and homesick. My wood work has all been painted white, my walls ivory with cream ceilings, my floors freshly varnished and waxed. I have gotten a gay linoleum for my kitchen floor, and blue and yellow china lends a festive air to my glassdoored cupboard, so that I am as cozy and comfortable as possible. The deep snow and bitter weather, reports of which have frightened my family, only makes me feel the cozier in contrast as my fire burns warmly and my radio brings me the day's news, good music and amusement as I will.

It has taken experience to convince me, and I cannot convince my dearest away friends, that I have no time here for loneliness. Even the holidays have been so busily occupied that there has been no time for heartaches, only an overflowing of gratitude as I go along for the generosity shown my Navaho and me. Thanksgiving was spent helping the Missionary prepare and serve a Navaho feast. Wash tubs of mutton stew and potatoes, dishpans and dishpans of Mexican beans, miraculously multiplied loaves of bread, and gallons and gallons of the weakest coffee imaginable. Food supplied by the Government.

Friends from home sent me money, clothing, quantities of toys, candy and nuts for a Christmas celebration, and I contributed them all to the Missionary's Christmas tree. I found he was expecting about five hundred Navaho for a two-day celebration—a Christmas Tree on Christmas Eve, a feast on Christmas Day. The Government again furnished food for the feast, but whether from insufficient funds or inadequate planning, preparations for the tree were pitifully scant. With my funds and supplies

8. Marion Gilmore, Forster's first cousin, lived in California.

to the rescue we popped corn, made popcorn balls, polished apples, filled bags, inflated balloons, arranged toys and gay bandannas until the tree (which Grant had brought from the nearby mountainside and trimmed, with my trimmings augmenting last year's left-overs) began to assume a festive air. For days, Navaho known and strange, had been coming to me ostensibly for "aze" (medicine) but in reality to get me to show them "Kismas" on my calendar. Carefully noting the intervening days on their fingers they signified an intention to return on its Eve. With such an air of anticipation abroad I could but redouble my efforts to make the event worthwhile. When at length the day arrived and the church doors opened the hideous little building was filled to bursting. The Missionary had collected a group of returned students to act as choir, and they sang, unaccompanied and largely out of tune, a number of appropriate and inappropriate hymns—one for the edification of the congregation translated into Navaho, "Nonny Ho Gee" (Jesus is Calling). Lilly sang a solo, which seems to be her long suit. I am told she did it at her own wedding here at the Mission some three years ago, gowned in lavender lace from Montgomery Ward's. Grant, coached by the Missionary, preached our Christmas sermon and I regretted my lack of Navaho.

Heaven knows where these people all spent the night. My building, upstairs and down, the church and basement, several sheds and the garage were filled and overflowing, but they couldn't have accommodated one-tenth of that mob. Next morning I was awakened early by the crackle of fire and the chatter of voices just beneath my window and began the day's fun by tossing out cigarettes and watching the ensuing scramble.

Having postponed my Christmas dinner until Sunday, I spent that day preparing a traditional feast which a box from home provided, and my several tables combined scarcely seated my guests—the three Missionaries and the three Benallys (the Missionary's interpreter's family). Next morning at daybreak came a rap at my door and Grant's agitated voice calling "Miss Forster, Lilly think's she's going to have a baby!" Alack, my Christmas feast had proved too much for Lilly, and the baby whom she expected several weeks hence was on its way.

Dressing with speed, I hurried over to Grant's little house to find that it was too late to think of taking Lilly thirty miles to the hospital for her delivery, as I had meant to do. I had to face the prospect of delivering her alone under what seemed most unfavorable conditions. I set about getting a fire made, water boiling and other necessary preparations, watching Lilly meanwhile. Difficulties threatened and I was relieved when the

Trader sent word that he had his car out and was ready to start for the doctor at a word from me.[9] I gave the word and he was off. In spite of haste, however, it was several hours before he could get back (bad roads, and the doctor operating when he reached the hospital), so that Lilly and I managed alone and the stork arrived with a husky Navaho boy just before the doctor got there.

9. In an early draft of these letters, Forster notes that the missionary refused to send his car for the doctor. "The gentleman sent back word that he didn't think the doctor would come and he thought anyhow I could manage alone!"

Red Rock
January 1, 1932

Dear Laura:

My last letter telling you of our Christmas celebration omitted an incident which I withheld lest you think me foolhardy and grow anxious—your habit. Since it terminated amicably I am now willing to share it. You will remember that weather and roads made travel difficult for some time before Christmas so that I depended on the Trader and the Missionary for communication with Shiprock and the Agency. About December 20th the Missionary went in to arrange with the Agent for food for his Christmas feast. On his return he told me that the Agency was sending him some clothing for distribution, so when a great truck load arrived a day or two later I sent the driver to his house and he had the generous supply of ex-army coats, socks and blankets stored in an empty room down the hall from mine. The door was locked and he said he would make the distribution after his Tree party. I, of course, attended the party, and then repairing to my rooms immediately found myself maintaining open house for numerous friends and acquaintances. While this impromptu sociability was in progress I was surprised to have Grant appear at my door with a message from the Missionary that I was supposed to be distributing the clothing. Leaving my guests I went down the hall through a milling crowd of excited and somewhat noisy Indians to find the door to the storeroom locked. Pursuit of the Missionary found him retired to his house in a state as excited as that of the Indians. He said yes the distribution was my business—the things had been sent to me. I replied that this was the first I had heard of it but that I certainly would not shirk a duty. He produced the key and borrowing his interpreter I went back to begin the job. Before opening the door I told Grant to ask the Indians to come to me in order, explaining that I wanted to give each man his need but that as the supply was limited and my acquaintance with them slight I must rely on them to make their requests reasonably. It was soon evident that in their excited state this would not be possible and when they began to crowd the room uncomfortably, pushing and grabbing from each other (tho loathe and slow), I realized that the Christmas festivities had been attended on the side by the demon Rum—or its Navaho equivalent. My reaction to this realization was quick enough, I think, to save me from an unpleasant hour or two. I planted myself before the store of warm clothing which I knew they needed and wanted and had Grant say for me that I could give them nothing until they were sober enough to tell me the truth about their needs. If the situation had not been as it was I think I might have been amused at the surprised consternation on the faces before me. As it was, sympathy moved me to reiterate that when they could come to my door sober I would have the key and together we would select necessities. Afterthought and calm consideration convince me that my attitude was perhaps not a wise one in dealing with intoxication and that the character and good sense of the Navaho prevented further unpleasantness. My days since have been largely given to the promised distribution.

A happy sequel to my Christmas which promises to add efficiency to my efforts has appeared in the form of a young English-speaking Navaho who, hearing of my need of an interpreter thinks he would like the job. The small allowance by the Association for an interpreter's services, doubled by other funds, seems shamefully inadequate to me but apparently spells wealth to him, and as soon as he can find a place to live nearby he will begin his duties. Timothy is his name and I think Timothy and I will like each other. He has a wife and two small boys who I met at the Christmas party. Timothy is responsive to friendly advances and his history has been confidently related during our several interviews. He was born and grew up in this neighborhood, so his intimacy with the people hereabouts will be a great advantage to me. As a small boy he was taken into the boarding school at Shiprock where he pursued the white man's education for some five or six years. Then he had an accident which resulted in the loss of two fingers and an interrupted education was never resumed. His wife is a Navaho girl whom he knew in school and they have been living in the vicinity of her home on a mesa beyond Farmington. Hard times and a Navaho custom which will not admit a girl's husband to her mother's hogan have driven him to seek refuge with his relatives. With borrowed horse and wagon they made their move just before Thanksgiving and were caught in the terrific blizzard which kept desert dwellers house bound for days. Their way was made across the desert in as straight a line as Timothy could steer, without regard for road. The cold was so severe Timothy's heart was torn by the suffering of his little children. He gave them his overcoat for warmth and he ran beside the horse with nothing warmer than a cotton shirt to shield him from the bitter wind. His overcoat and Ethel's blanket shawl saved the three in the wagon from death by freezing. The story, graphically told,

Timothy Kellywood and his family, 1932

opens my understanding to the suffering and needs of my Navaho neighbors. The things we would consider the barest and poorest necessities would spell more than comfort and luxury to them. My food and shelter, coat and coal begin to hurt and weigh upon my spirits. What can I do to help them?

Red Rock
January 16, 1932

Dear Laura:

Have I told you that I am having clinics once a week with a doctor out from the hospital? The weather is so cold and my people have to come from such distances that I am preparing and serving soup for them, and my dispensary, warmed by a cheerful wood fire and advertising my soup in odoriferous fashion, is a popular place on clinic day. I strongly suspect many of them come for soup and not from need to see the doctor. I am, however, by means of this bait catching a good many cases which would not otherwise come to us for care, cases of trachoma, diseased tonsils, chronic appendicitis, etc. And the other day I had a visit from John Billy. Do you remember meeting him at Mr. Morris' camp last fall? I was shocked at the change in his appearance. He had lost many pounds and his prominent eyes and extreme nervous symptoms gave clear indication of his condition, so I persuaded him to return to clinic and he is now in the hospital recovering satisfactorily from an operation for exopthalmic goitre.

You will be glad to know that Timothy is on daily duty with me. Timothy seems a treasure, apparently knows every road and hogan in our district, drives well, is careful of the car and considerate of my comfort. I should say that Timothy's talent is for friendship. Wherever we go we meet his friends and I believe he is making them mine. He is sympathetic and pitiful to suffering in patients, and sensitively appreciative of the beauty we encounter on the trips we make about this gorgeous countryside together, so that I am fast becoming fond of him as well as dependent on his services. He seems very young, but is twenty-two. Ethel, his wife, is a dear, too, and I feel that I have made an altogether happy connection.

Besides acting as chauffeur, guide and mouthpiece for me, Timothy is proving invaluable in many ways. Imagine the comfort, after weeks of arduous and conflicting housekeeping duties, of having some one to carry coal, empty ashes, chop kindling, shake rugs, sweep my dispensary and carry water for me! And Ethel will do my laundry.

Red Rock
February 18, 1932

Dear Marion:

Your long and interesting letter deserved an early answer, but when you hear how I have been occupied you will not wonder that it didn't get it. Laura made me an unexpected, happy visit from January 23rd to February 15th, and you may imagine how the days flew. I've had two other guests (several days each), have had Flu myself and am in the midst of an epidemic which keeps me very busy. My life is far from the lonely monotonous one I feared I would find in so isolated a spot, and I find myself wishing very constantly for you to share it with me. I am hoping, however, that a vacation may bring you my way some day. I believe you might find material here for writing if you are still so inclined. Would that I had a glib pen and time to use it! Some of my experiences this winter have been thrilling to me and I believe are sufficiently unusual to be interesting to people who know nothing of the Navajos, or of desert life.

One day while Laura was with me we braved the elements, Timothy driving, and plowed through snowdrifts to town to bring home two of our patients whom we were sure were ready and anxious to leave the hospital. While waiting for the mail to get in before we started back, we were surprised to have Grant drive up evidently in great haste. He had followed us thirty miles to town to tell me that a woman living about eight miles from the Mission had sent for me. She had been in labor for five days and was desperate. She had twice previously been delivered by the Mission doctor with instruments and had lost her baby each time. It all sounded sufficiently serious, and I dispatched Timothy and Laura homewards with the two patients we had come to fetch and I went with Grant and the doctor, after outfitting at the hospital with the necessary instruments and supplies. I must admit that my courage quailed when I contemplated the prospect of an instrumental delivery in a Navaho hogan, and throughout the trip I hoped desperately against hope that we might find the baby safely arrived or that we might be able to take the woman to the hospital. The difficulty of transportation over the road we travelled, however, discouraged the latter hope and the former was, of course, futile. The road to the hogan was obliterated and we stuck repeatedly in drifts, so that it took us four hours to reach our destination. It was then

Hogan near Red Rock, winter, 1932

dark and we found the fire-lit hogan filled with sympathetic friends whom we speedily dispersed, keeping only the husband and another relative to help. Navaho hogans are devoid of furniture of any description, but we managed to secure from a neighboring hogan two wooden fruit boxes which we utilized as operating table. This elevated our patient only about six or eight inches, so it was necessary to work squatting on the dirt floor. Bottles of ready prepared soap and water, lysol solution, surgical alcohol, etc., with plenty of sterile towels, sheets, sponges and dressings were arranged as conveniently as possible to aid and guard our technique. While I prepared the patient and the doctor opened and arranged packages, Grant must extinguish the fire before we could start the ether. We were therefore left without light except that supplied by my small two-battery flash, which Grant operated, directing the light first to me as I administered ether, then to the doctor busy with his instruments. Back and forth, back and forth darted the tiny light as we cried our need, and I prayed for a steady hand between flashes. Imagine our surprise and delight when we heard the lusty cry of a living and evidently husky baby. After five days labor! The family certainly considered that we had "made magic" and we left a happy and grateful father and a quietly resting mother a little later, just as Timothy arrived, breathless with excitement, at the hogan door. "What did you come for, Timothy?" I asked. "To help get that baby out," said Timothy, and he has not yet forgiven Fate that he was not in time.

Another struggle through snowdrifts and we were home for a ten o'clock supper which Laura had cooked and was keeping warm for us. We found her wearing dark glasses, which we always wear when we go abroad in the sunlight and snow, and when I asked if her eyes were bothering her she disgustedly snatched them off saying "I *wondered* why the light was so dim." Never was a supper so good, never bed more welcome.

More snow before morning and a strong wind piling up huge drifts made it utterly impossible to reach my mother and babe next day, but on the third day I managed to secure a horse and rode eight miles to find them snug and comfortable in their tiny hogan, almost buried in the snow. Cautioning the family to get the message to me should untoward symptoms arise, I left a small present of clothing for the baby and retraced my horse's footsteps through the snow. It was a glorious world I rode through. The darkly wooded mountains and deeply colored rocks toward which I faced lent blue shadow and opalescent tints to the unbroken expanse of glistening snow which stretched before them, and my heart lifted and sang with joy in the sheer beauty which met my eyes on every hand.

Red Rock
February 20th, 1932

Dear Emily:

Life is proving strenuous just now with a Flu epidemic in progress and every effort to reach patients made difficult and prolonged by roads and weather, so that I reach home lazily inclined to stretch and bask beside my fire with book or radio to enhance the contrast to the world outside. I must take "time out," however, to tell you of my recent trip to Santa Fe.

When I found that Laura must leave last week and that she wanted to go home by way of Santa Fe I decided to drive her that far, or rather to have Timothy drive us and, when we discovered that Mrs. Francis longs avidly to see the world, we invited her to go with us. She is an excellent weaver but Navaho designs have so deteriorated with the demands of our American market that I long to show my weaver friends the beautiful blankets collected in the Laboratory of Anthropology in Santa Fe and so renew old ideals and simplify the elaborations which our Trading Posts display.[10] This seemed an opportunity. Imagine the preparation which began in her little home—indeed our whole community was astir with interest and perhaps a little envy. The night before our early start she ran over to show us she was ready, and *did* she shine? Timothy, too, was all agog with excitement as he had never been beyond Gallup.

Next morning no one of us, not even drowsy Laura, dared oversleep, and we were off before sunrise, to be overtaken a few miles from home by a flat tire! Timothy, whom nothing daunts, made a rapid change and we were off again on our grand adventure. Gallup, with its locomotives clanging in and out, its rows of houses and paved streets, was strange and exciting enough, but Laura's happy recollection of a zoo in Albuquerque was a real inspiration. The occasion proved too much for Timothy's English vocabulary and he lapsed into Navaho with Mrs. Francis, but Laura and I were content to watch their faces and begrudged no minute of the time thus spent. Buffalo and bears, elk, deer, monkeys and fowls of various variety created excited comment and curious study, but Timothy's amazement passed all bound with his first glimpse of an ostrich which he

10. The Laboratory of Anthropology housed the collections of the Indian Arts Fund, a Santa Fe organization devoted to the preservation of fine examples of post-Conquest American Indian art. Many members of the organization were also involved with the New Mexico Association on Indian Affairs, Forster's employer.

Mrs. Francis, 1932

called a big chicken. His eyes fairly leaped from their sockets and I am sure he tried to pinch himself awake. It was beyond his belief. Mrs. Francis' joy was supremely climaxed when in the next pen a gorgeous peacock, as though on signal, spread his tail and strutted for our admiration. Nothing had prepared her for such unexpected beauty and her face was touchingly eloquent.

On our way once more, I inquired through Timothy if she were getting hungry and she replied that with the glories of Albuquerque behind and Santa Fe ahead she had no time to recognize appetite. Arrived in Santa Fe we put them in an Auto Camp cottage for the night and next day we spent reveling in the beauties of Indian craft at the Laboratory. Mr. Nusbaum and Dr. Mera spent several generous hours showing us beautiful specimens of blankets from the vaults and Mrs. Francis and Timothy were entranced.[11] Timothy repeated again and again in awed wonder, "We've heard about the old blankets but we sure didn't know that they were as beautiful as this," and Mrs. Francis touched them all with careful fingers, very evidently making a quiet study of texture and weave, color and design. I am anxious to see the result of such inspiration in her weaving hereafter.

It happened that that day was Deric Nusbaum's nineteenth birthday and Mrs. Nusbaum invited Laura and me to a celebration dinner.[12] We were loath to leave our Navaho friends to the unaccustomed intricacies of a restaurant meal alone and were about to refuse reluctantly when she, seeing our hesitation, hastened to assure us that they were included in the invitation. Wasn't that sweet of her? Their behavior throughout the party was amazing. Timothy's instinctive appreciation of beauty (of which that house is full!) and his quick response to friendliness made him a delightful guest, and Mrs. Francis fairly dazzled us with her amazing poise and dignity. Having no table, she is, I am sure, unaccustomed to table ware and had first met knives and forks and china plates at my house several weeks before, but she bore herself bravely when we were seated to a fairly formal dinner of several courses, with what must have

11. Jesse Nusbaum (1887–1975) was director of the Laboratory of Anthropology, and Dr. Harry P. Mera (1875–1951) was chairman of the Indian Arts Fund.

12. Forster and Gilpin had met Aileen Nusbaum, Jesse's wife, in 1924, and in 1925 Gilpin photographed the summer Indian pageant she staged at Mesa Verde National Park.

seemed a multiplicity of forks, knives, and spoons. Without the slightest self-consciousness she frankly watched the rest of us and invariably chose the proper implement. With shining eyes she watched the fun and laughter which filled the evening, and when we left she bade Timothy say that her only regret was her lack of English and consequent inability to join the fun.

Red Rock
February [?], 1932

Dear Laura:

It was a rather doleful party which left you in Santa Fe. When Timothy remarked pathetically "We sure are lonesome" I roused myself to cheer us as best I might, and soon Timothy was chuckling "I know somebody who is nineteen years and one day old!" From that he drifted into the duck story again and soon he and Mrs. Francis were engaged in conversation which I longed to be able to understand. She was positively loquacious for a Navaho lady and from the amount of animation on both sides I judged they were reminiscing happily. Finally Timothy sighed in English, "I sure wish we's going back to Santa Fe to see those folks," and I laughed to myself at not being able to escape "folks" even in Navaho land.

We stopped in Albuquerque at the school, where Timothy found his friends. I had discovered that our breakfast was inadequate according to Navaho standards, so we stopped again at a restaurant where Timothy and Mrs. Francis appeased insulted appetites—and arrived in Gallup at one-thirty. Along the way Timothy collected a tall cactus and a piece of lava to illustrate future stories. In Gallup we left the car to be greased while we lunched at the Harvey counter. While we were thus engaged a train pulled in and we excused ourselves to the haughty and unsympathetic lady who was serving us and repaired to the platform to see the sight.

After lunch I found that Timothy longed to see a "show", gently hinting that Mrs. Francis was curious. Since we had no choice we saw Greta Garbo in *Mata Hari*. Timothy apparently understood almost as little as Mrs. Francis, who admitted that she was "scared" but glad to have another wonder to recount. At four-thirty we were on the road again and as we neared home Mrs. Francis produced some highly scented talcum powder which she used with telling effect! I learned that she had sold a saddle blanket in Santa Fe for two dollars, which accounted for numerous packages.

At my door Timothy tried touchingly to thank me for the trip and "for treating us so nice." When I thought he was gone he ran back to say "Don't be too lonely, Miss Forster."

I had hardly gotten in when Lilly called to hear the news and stayed until I nearly fell asleep in my chair. When she did leave she borrowed my "spare" lamp which I haven't seen since.

Dick's sister came in this afternoon to get me to help her make a voluminous Navvy skirt—black with orange ruffle edged with red! Twenty-five patients during the day.

Timothy's mother, Lukachukai, 1933

Red Rock
February 27, 1932

Dear Laura:

Your visit to us, so filled with eager interest in the small happenings of Red Rock life, has made Timothy and me want to continue to share them with you. Many times a day Timothy voices the belief that you would enjoy this or that, and I have started numerous letters to you which have been so interrupted that they have degenerated into a series of notes of daily doings, which herewith I submit:

February 18.

Timothy and I are fighting sore throats (our own and others). The Trader has been in bed for two days with a temperature of 101. Late yesterday a messenger brought us news that John Billy is sick, and in spite of the Trader's opinion that it was impossible Timothy and I made an effort to reach his hogan this morning. We passed the hogans of Jim Ferryboat and Jimmy Yazi and stopped for gossip at both. The Yazis have recovered health and Jim Ferryboat was much interested at the prospect of hearing Mrs. Nusbaum's Navaho stories. His daughter doesn't think she wants to teach me to weave and his wife doesn't wish to part with some very disreputable teeth. Jimmy Yazi elected to ride along with us until we got stuck in a wash, which repetition of our last ride together seemed to amuse him very much. Timothy's usual optimism was dampened by the thought of numerous washes ahead and the amount of digging and pushing it took us to get out of this one, so we discouragedly turned back, asking Jimmy Yazi to relay a message to John Billy.

February 20.

Yesterday morning I was waked at dawn by Grant knocking at my door. I tried to answer but found that I had no voice, so I grabbed my bathrobe and went out to find Nachene Benally, who had come for me because his boy was very sick. I sent him for Timothy while I hurried into my clothes, and we set out. After driving about five miles we climbed on foot a mile so steep that I was breathless when we reached the hogan, in which we found a very, very sick lad—another ruptured appendix. The father, two brothers and Timothy, each at the corner of a blanket, carried him down the precipitous trail and we took him to the hospital for operation. I have had no news since. We reached home about noon, hungry for the combination breakfast and lunch which Mrs. Francis appeared in time to enjoy with me. For the first time I caught her in a breach of table etiquette. In her amusement over some sally of mine she thrust out her tongue and wiped her knife on it. Timothy and I spent most of the afternoon sitting stupidly by the kitchen fire without much conversation and sympathizing with our throats. By night my temperature was 101.5, and I am spending this morning on the chaise longue, voiceless and achy, but not very ill. I am told by Grant that the Missionary is sick and Lilly under the weather, the Trader about the same. Timothy is feeling a little better but is pepless and discouraged over me. He is nicely thoughtful and anxious to save me in every possible way.

February 24.

After several wretched days I am feeling better. Everybody in our neighborhood is sick or recovering.

Yesterday Timothy and I drove over to his brother's, as we had heard the family was sick. We found them all better but I didn't regret the trip. I was entranced with the place. It is beautifully set, rather close to the mountains, with a view on one hand of the lovely red rocks and cliffs, and on the other a view of the desert towards Shiprock. He has a nice rock-built house with a splendid bough-covered shelter on one side. Near the house is his farm, fence enclosed (something like John Low's only closer built), and on it is a nice pond, spring fed. Beyond this lie his orchard and a great alfalfa field. He has some horses, cows, sheep, and a few goats. Doesn't that make an idyllic picture? He showed me his Yeibichai costume. The black loin cloth is elaborately trimmed with my Christmas ribbons and a woolen fringe at the bottom which he wishes to adorn further with little tinkly bells. I promised to ask you to get some for me—about a dozen, I should think.

Today Timothy has gone to bed in my dispensary with a temperature of 102.5. Aching and miserable, he is wrapped in blankets with a cold wash cloth on his brow and a pitcher of lemonade on the table beside him, and is the picture of forlorn invalidism, very grateful for small attentions.

I am painting dozens of throats daily and dispensing quantities of Flu remedies.

February 26.

Timothy is better today, temperature not above 99.5 so far. Have had to make two trips today without him, one to see Lee's wife and three-day-old baby. Mary went with me and to my surprise (I hadn't suspected friendship there) she shyly presented me with a nice ring.

I decided it wouldn't hurt Timothy to come up to supper and to listen to the radio. Before supper was over Grant dropped in. A little later came Eugene to hear Amos and Andy, and later still Francis and Mrs. Francis. After Amos and Andy, I sent Timothy back to bed and Grant and Eugene left, but the others have just gone and at ten-thirty I must wash supper dishes. I find the Francises are Catholic and Francis has borrowed *Death Comes for the Archbishop*.

Red Rock
March 10, 1932

Dear Laura:

Our weather has moderated marvelously and the snow is fast disappearing from the desert but remains near the mountains. Timothy and I are getting about to hogans more, and since the days are still short it is often dark before we get home. At such times Timothy loses his self-consciousness and tells me entertaining stories of his childhood and sometimes sings Navaho songs for my delight. They are really quite lovely, surprisingly varied in tone when one hears them individually. Timothy declares (and he sounds truthful) that he doesn't know the meaning of the words.

I had heard nothing from John Billy since our attempted visit and decided yesterday to try again, and this time we reached his hogan. John Billy is evidently suffering from a hangover from the Flu and I thought it wise to take him to the doctor for an examination. He demurred, but I told him I intended to take him if I had to use a rope. He laughed at this and repeated it to his wife. John Billy, you know, is a Carlisle graduate but his wife has never been to school and doesn't speak English. I have fallen in love with her. Her face is very expressive and she has a happy sense of humor. When John Billy went into his hogan to prepare to accompany me she followed him and presently appeared leading him on a rope which she handed to me. The giggles which we enjoyed together over this joke sealed our friendship.

When we got home we found several patients waiting for "aze," amongst them a nice old man with the kindest and most benignant of faces. He is Timothy's uncle—Killed-A-White-Man by name. He wanted liniment, and when I told him through Timothy that I had none he glared sternly and inquired why I was not supplied with the things a nurse was supposed to have. Whereupon I pretended to tremble and asked fearfully if he had ever killed a white woman. His eyes began to twinkle and we parted friends, in spite of my reprehensible slackness in the matter of medicinal supplies. Timothy is reticent about the manner in which his ancient uncle acquired his name, but Grant tells the story with gusto. He says that many years ago when this old man was young he went out on a hunting expedition one day with his two brothers (Timothy's father and another). They were armed with bows and arrows and hunted all day without success. Towards the end of the day they came upon a white man who was camping and was well supplied with food and drink ("*wine* in a *jug*"). They were hungry and thirsty and waited for the man to offer refreshment. This he failed to do and when they finally proffered a request and were refused Killed-A-White-Man drew bow and earned his name.

Red Rock
March 27, 1932

Dear Emily:

Letter writing has been difficult of late because I have so little
uninterrupted time. My radio, goldfish, magazines, checkers, and cards
attract guests almost every evening when I am at home, and Sunday is
invariably full also. I have not, however, outgrown the feeling that Sunday
is a more or less free day, and this morning I lay rather late abed—to
regret it later. Before my breakfast was ready Jack came in and challenged
me in eloquent sign language to a game of checkers. He is an insatiable
player and we played on and on until I was starved, so at ten o'clock I
shooed him out and had some breakfast. I was still at my dishwashing
when Timothy and Ethel came in with the children, followed shortly by
Mrs. Francis and Mary. Later came Nachene Benally's wife and small son.
They wanted news of the boy I took to the hospital with a ruptured
appendix some time ago, and I was happily able to give them the best of
reports. By this time my room was growing crowded and as it was lovely
and warm outside we moved on to the porch where we sat Navaho
fashion in the sun! By and by Lilly joined us, and after a whispered
conversation with Mary she said to me "Mary wants to tell you
something." "Tell away," said I. "By yourself," said Lilly, so we repaired to
privacy where Mary, between giggles, announced her engagement to
Yellow Mexican's son. I was, of course, enthusiastically congratulatory and
promised a wedding gift and learned that Mary covets a coffee pot and
cups. Lilly departed and the Ute Woman arrived with her spinning. I got
out my wool and cards.

Some time ago I decided that I would get my friends to teach me to
card, spin, and weave as all Navaho women do, thinking that they would
be readier to learn some things from me if they were teaching me
something in return, so I bought wool from the Trader, washed it
carefully and am now trying to learn to card. Each of my friends has to
show me her own particular method and all must laugh at my awkward
efforts. It is lots of fun and we have gay times at it. From time to time
one guest would leave, another come, and I began to fear I should have
no chance to dine that day as I simply could not stretch my larder to feed
that crowd. It at last thinned to Mrs. Francis and the Ute Woman and we
hied us to the kitchen and prepared a feast. Mrs. Ute was at first dubious
about my grapefruit, but if she finally left anything but the skin you'd

Mary weaving on outdoor loom, Red Rock, 1933

have needed a microscope to find it! Poor old Hastin Nez had been hanging around all day on the edge of our crowd looking hungry and I wanted to invite him to our party but neither of my guests would agree, so I am haunted by his wistful face.

So the day has gone and I have been thinking of you "aside" all day and wanting an opportunity to write, and now I find I am too tired to write anything worth while!

Next day: Yesterday and today make me rejoice that Spring is surely on its way! It has been a cruel winter for my Navaho friends and death has taken toll of man and beast. We are told of a little child who was frozen to death in a distant hogan while its mother was out herding sheep. We have taken several cases of very badly frozen feet to the hospital and I have treated many less severe cases in my dispensary. Pneumonia has been rife and one small mite died in its mother's arms in the Trader's car as we struggled through the snow to the hospital. Timothy and I were out one afternoon with Jimmy Yazi in an attempt to reach his hogan where his family was sick with Flu. Breaking a road through the snow we inadvertently ran one wheel into a deep buried arroyo. After vainly struggling until dark to get out we abandoned the car until next day and tramped home through deep snow. As I was preparing for bed, Timothy reappeared at my door with a man who had evidently travelled far and fast to seek our services. He was bathed in sweat and looked exhausted. He said his baby was very sick and would I come? Of course I would—but how? An appeal to the Trader found him willing, as always, to help, and I was more than glad to have his added strength and judgment to help us over the difficult road that lay before us. The little baby we found sick, indeed, and the parents unexpectedly willing to take it to the hospital, which I felt sure was the only possible chance of saving the little life, and that but a faint hope. Can you picture our struggle through the snow, sticking in drifts, digging and pushing out, sticking again, digging again, pushing again, while the mother on the back seat held a little form in its Navaho cradle close to her heart under her blanket? We had nearly reached the hospital when, alarmed at the cessation of the pitiful wail that had distressed our ears throughout the trip, I asked the Trader to stop, and we found, as I had feared, that the little life was gone. The body was left at the Hospital by the grief stricken parents for burial, but they took the tiny cradle in which it had been strapped with them and when we were out again amongst the snowdrifts on the moonlit desert they asked us to stop. Their baby's cradle must never be used for living babe again, so it was left to the mercy of the elements—a "chindi" cradle.

Red Rock
March 30, 1932

Dear Marion:

Your somewhat delayed letter reminds me that in my last to you I told you of the little baby born in a hogan, and from the story I am now about to recount I fear you will think that I jump with undue celerity from borning to burying. Let me hasten to say that had the Missionary been at home I should gladly have turned the latter job over to him, but as he was away I could not in kindness refuse my services. I am hoping that you will not find in the tale material for unholy mirth. I certainly "rose" to the occasion and did my feeble best.

One morning recently I was enjoying a delicious pre-rising nap when I was roused by a rap on my door. There I found Timothy with a man who had walked some eight miles to bespeak our services in the matter of burying an old lady who had died in the night. The man, of course, was hungry after his long walk, and Timothy unfed, so I prepared breakfast for us all, and we then collected some old planks, sawed them the proper length for a coffin, put them in the car with hammer and nails, and set out. Arrived at the old woman's home we nailed the box together and were ready to proceed. The family had moved out of the hogan and was hovering over a fire at some distance. They produced yards and yards of green chambric, a new lavender cotton blanket, an army blanket (which I recognized as one I had given the old lady for Christmas), and some newly tanned buckskin—all of which we were expected to use for the burial. Nothing must be removed from the body, which was garbed in its habitual clothing with all the jewelry the old lady possessed. When our undertaking duties were accomplished we were ready to prepare the grave. After some conversation with the family Timothy announced that they wished to bury her in the hogan but feared I might object since they knew it was contrary to white custom. Knowing that the hogan in which death has occurred is invariably deserted and never used again, I saw no reason for objection—in fact I rather approved the sentiment—so Timothy and the son-in-law began the difficult task of digging a grave in the hard-packed hogan floor. When it was finally deep enough to serve we managed to get the box in, and then, my dear, to my vast amazement and utter horror, the family (much too well informed of white custom) requested me to "say something." Consider the circumstances and tell me what you would have said? My bedazed brain leaped wildly from "Now I

Lay Me" to "Dust Thou Art to Dust returneth was not written of the Soul," and I finally managed to ask the two English speaking members of the congregation if they could say the Lord's Prayer. They were reassuringly doubtful so I announced that we would say it anyway. The box was then covered with sheepskins and the grave filled. Then came the nailing up of the hogan door, the closing of the opening in the top, and our old lady was left to rest in the home where she had spent happy years.

According to Navaho belief, it takes a soul four days to enter this life, four days to leave it, so the family must for four days remain nearby, moving then to the west.

As we were about to leave I wondered at Timothy's delay until he beckoned me to where he stood watching a herd of sheep. The old lady's daughter, wishing to make us a present, waded into the heart of the herd and dragged out first a sheep and then a goat which she slaughtered before my unwilling eyes, and we must accept the carcasses. Timothy was in no way loath!

Red Rock
April 3, 1932

Dear Emily:

Spring in our country is proving more than proverbially variable. It is at times deliciously warm and tempts us to tripping about to hogans, not only in visits to patients but to enjoy the sight of the young lambs and goats gamboling with the joy of new life and the irresponsibility of babyhood. Timothy's delight in them is as keen as mine and we could hang over corral fences for hours were leisure unlimited. The lambs are amusingly long-legged and awkward, the little goats adorably animated and graceful, and who could resist their entertaining antics? I am beginning to understand the Navaho's busy-ness at lambing time. All about the corrals we see deep pits dug in the sand, with sometimes a mother sheep and just-born twins demonstrating their use. The other day we watched a small shepherd drive home a herd of ewes from pasture to a corral full of baby lambs. Three Navaho women stood within and handed out to each mother her baby or babies in turn. It was amazing how they recognized relationship. An occasional mistake created comic panic until the proper connection was made and peace restored. With warm days shearing begins, and comedy and pathos are blended as the creatures submit to the shearing with an air of utter martyrdom but emerge from the shearer's hands insultedly indignant. The babies are bewildered and they need mother's voice to establish her identity.

At other times, when the wind blows, driving the sand before it in clouds, only necessity drags us from within doors. Sometimes it blows for days at a time with diabolic fury and persistence, and the strain on our nerves is tense beyond belief. An occasional lapse into last winter's habit with a fall of snow overnight settles wind and sand to our delight and we look forward again to sunshine and fair weather.

When we are kept indoors I have a multiplicity of duties to keep me occupied. Besides my housekeeping (which is more arduous here than anywhere I have lived) and small jobs of darning and mending, there are my dispensary supplies to be kept up, fresh solutions to be made, remedies compounded from drugs on hand, returned bottles to be sterilized and washed, and countless other small but necessary duties which must be sandwiched between the attention given patients who come to my dispensary. It is harder to keep Timothy occupied, but he has recently acquired a Montgomery Ward catalogue over which he pores

Group in corral, 1932

when leisure offers, and he has just closed it with a wistful sigh and the generous offer, "Anybody else want to look at the wishing book?"

I have had lately a case which necessitates a fifteen mile drive each day over a road which makes me tremble for my car and takes constant toll from tires. We rarely get home without a fresh rock cut. My patient is a darling wee thing (a picture in her tiny velvet blouse and long full skirt, a diminutive replica of her mother's costume) who is just learning to walk and who in her first proud attempts about the hogan fell, thrusting both little hands into the open fire. The dressing has been painful and the little thing began, quite naturally, to hate me and to indulge in vicious scolding whenever I appeared. The family was evidently much amused by her tirades and I have just learned that she has been calling me an old fox— the most insulting epithet used by the Navahos. The treatment grows daily less painful and we are progressing to friendship, encouraged on my part by the gift of a small toy.

Navaho woman and child in hogan, 1932

Red Rock
April 10, 1932

Dear [no name provided]:

Now is the time of wind. It roars and rumbles, shrieks and whistles round my house and I shrink and shiver and dread any necessity to face its blast. The air is red and so dense with sand that the Post at the foot of the hill is no longer visible. The little wouldbe cottonwoods before my window writhe and twist and sweep the ground with their tops but cling against uprooting. What a persistent hold they have on life, and what a graceless life it is! My windows I keep tight closed but when I wake in the morning the sills are inch deep in sand and a red dust cloudfollows my foot as I cross my room. I must use a dustpan in lieu of a shovel before I wield my broom. Ah, the joys of desert life.

But what a shameful wail! What right have I to complain? I am secure in comfort while all around me families are herded close in tiny hogans which though proof, 'tis true, from the wind and sand are devoid of convenience and generally crowded far past comfort. The necessity of tending their flocks takes many abroad. My own unavoidable excursions have taught me the cruel sting of wind-driven sand to skin and eye and I do not find it surprising that denizens of the desert suffer from trachoma. From these storms I have learned to value the comfort of the Navaho shawls.

A period like this when hardship and want, discomfort and suffering press close around me stirs my mind to unhappy wonder. Whose the fault? These people do really live in the same land of plenty with their white "brothers." Time was, no doubt, when their own portion of this wielded as generous a living as they know but a great increase in numbers and no space or chance for expansion have resulted in a pitiful paucity of living requisites. The Navaho, as are other Indians in New Mexico and Arizona, are wards of our Government. Does that not mean that our Government is responsible for their welfare? Must they live in such discomfort as would surely distress the most callous? Must they die each winter from cold and hunger? As I sit by the fire and listen to the voice of the bitter wind I wonder at the blytheness of spirit that has filled our pleasant weather.

The Missionary doesn't seem to understand his Delco plant very well and we are frequently without water and lights. I have been melting snow lately to save carrying water from the spring in the wash at the foot of the hill and have gotten two good kerosene lamps, so you see I am becoming independent of the luxuries of modern civilization.

The difficulty of housing Timothy and his family conveniently near has been solved by Francis offering his little house while he lives temporarily on better grazing ground for his sheep. As soon as weather and roads permit, Timothy will haul logs and build himself a hogan.

Red Rock
May 18, 1932

Dear Emily:

With the advent of mild weather and the business of lambing and shearing keeping my Navahos at home, work has grown slack for me, and Saturday afternoon I accepted a naive invitation from Timothy to take him and Woody prairie dog hunting. Ethel and the babies were eager for an outing too, so we all climbed into the Chevvy and set out over the desert. Timothy and Woody were armed with twenty-twos, with which they are uncannily expert, and the fat little prairie puppies, curiously interested in our movements, had small chance to escape their aim. Unfortunately the creatures were frequently poised on the brinks of their holes and when hit tumbled apparently into the bowels of the earth, whence Timothy's long arm was unable to extract them. When the boys' prowess had provided seventeen coveted carcasses for supper I persuaded them to leave some alive for the next shooting and we were off for home where Ethel prepared a feast for family and friends. Prairie dogs are a choice delicacy to the Navahos. They are drawn and cleaned, tossed on a bed of coals to burn off their hair, and roasted in their skins. Timothy threatens to present me with a cooked one and watch me eat it, but I am counting on his appetite and extreme fondness for prairie dog meat to counteract his generosity!

Next day, as Timothy had had reports that his mother, who lives across the mountains, was not well, we determined to make a crossing. Never shall I forget the beauty which greeted my eyes from that mountainside as we turned to look back at our home. To the north were unfolded red rock and cliff, monument and cavern, in rich and lovely hue; to the east spread the desert, bathed in delicate opalescent light, and in its midst Shiprock reared its height in breath-taking beauty. No other word describes the feeling with which one sees its lovely shape isolated on a desert which has become a very sea of color. Beyond, along the horizon, stretched dream-like mountains, shading from a hazy blue to a pink and creamlike white, and we were at once lost in happy ecstasy in contemplation of beauty which transcends description.

The mountain itself was gloriously green and we greeted as friends the mighty pines and clumps of scrub oak, the abundant fern and promise of flowers to come as summer advances—all a pleasant contrast to the desert's dearth of growth. The road we found soft in spots from recently melted snow, precipitous and rocky at times, but perfectly possible to traverse. Near the top a bobcat crossed the road ahead of us and sought shelter in a deep ravine on the other side. Again a bear ambled into the woods and stood on hind legs in evident curiousity to see us pass.

Descending the other side of the mountain we found ourselves in country surprisingly different from our own, a land embattled by towering red cliffs much more obtrusive in form and color than those with which we are familiar on our side.

Timothy's mother is a lovely creature and one does not wonder that when Timothy's father died she married a younger man and has now a flourishing second family. The present spouse is evidently what we know as a "moocher" and from all accounts labors diligently in an effort to secure the where-with-all for living for himself and family from his predecessor's family—Timothy and his two brothers. I fancy the story of his wife's alleged illness had been concocted by him and sent with the hope of securing food or money.

Timothy's mother instantly accepted me as a friend, thanking me with tears for making it possible for her son to so quickly travel thirty miles to see her. She gave me a lesson in weaving, at which she is expert, and urged frequent visits.

Red Rock
June 7, 1932

Dear Laura:

Yesterday Timothy and I spent a busy morning making hogan visits in one section of our district. We got home for a late lunch and while Timothy went home for his, I began the preparation of my own. Before it was completed Louise arrived to tell me that her brother's wife was about to have a baby. This family was new to our neighborhood and I had not met them, but Louise was sure they would welcome my services. I put the flag out for Timothy and set about my preparations for the occasion. Timothy was prompt in answering my summons and with Louise as a guide, we were soon on our way. We found the hogan filled with an audience of men, women, and children. The patient was held in a kneeling position by means of straps from the ceiling attached to each wrist. We were just too late for the actual delivery, but the old woman who seemed mistress of ceremonies accepted me as a pupil and showed me how things should be done. The little mother looked none too comfortable but I was not allowed to release her for rest until after the birth of the placenta. I was, however, allowed to do the umbilical dressing and rub the wee one with oil after which I was firmly bidden to hold it over a trough of sand prepared on the hogan floor while an attendant poured first cold then warm water over the little body, and the old lady rubbed it vigorously. You may believe it or not, but the result was a fresh pink-tan baby who was then dressed in swaddling bands with arms pinioned to its sides, as all good Navaho babies are, and laid in its mother's arms. While we were busy with the baby other assistants, under the old lady's direction, had prepared and given the mother crushed cedar foliage to smell and tea brew, therefrom to drink. We left peace in the little hogan in spite of the remaining audience of friends. I couldn't help wondering if there were still rites to follow, but if there were, I was not invited.

Timothy and I then went to see a patient about fifteen miles beyond this hogan, getting home at supper time to find a summons to take a dying girl to the hospital. This done, we reached home about ten-thirty glad to call it a day and ready to pray for an undisturbed night, which I am glad to say ensued. Today, Timothy and Mrs. Stolworthy being on my sick list, I have been dosing them with flu remedies, and attending to a succession of patients who have been able to come to me.

June 8th.

There was no chance to mail this but I hope to get to the post office tomorrow. My car must be greased again. It is hard to believe I have driven more than a thousand miles since I had it greased in Santa Fe. I have estimated that my mileage is averaging over a hundred miles a day, and that, when you realize that on days when I am kept busy at home with patients and dispensary, the car is unused, means long driving other days.

Timothy is having an orgy of company these days and finds it very hard to attend to his duties. My patience has been sorely tried this day, but I have long since learned that impatience gets one nowhere with the Navaho.

I must tell you that Louise brought Mrs. Navaho Jim—her aunt—to see me the other day. The old lady was delighted with the bits of shell you sent me some time ago and expects to make something beautiful of the ones I gave her. She stayed to lunch but when I produced eggs, intending to make an omelette, she signified her distaste so emphatically that I hastily opened a can of little sausages. These were hailed with delight. One is never in doubt here whether or not one's guests are pleased by one's menu! My salad was a curiosity and tolerated.

Red Rock
June 26, 1932

Dear Marion:

Summer is here at last and though the heat of the desert, unrelieved by shade, is somewhat severe we are at least spared the hardship of constant battle with snowdrifts. Our danger now is of getting stuck in the sand which abounds on every side, and later, I am told, come heavy rains and the danger of being stuck in mud or caught in "washes"—the sudden unexpected rush of waters in the dry sand creeks which traverse the desert. At present the roads hereabout are more possible to travel than at any time since I have been here and I am reveling in the beauty which I find in every direction.

Reports have been coming to us lately of sickness amongst the Navahos in the mountains. They are, you know, shepherds, and must move their herds as pasturage is exhausted. During the summer they leave the parched desert and find haven in the mountains where food is fresh and plentiful. To reach me means a long walk or horseback trip, so I decided to take my camping equipment and move for a day or two into the mountains myself in order to be available if really needed.

On Wednesday last we set out early in the afternoon, but overtaking a car in trouble and stopping to help, we were delayed and reached the place we had chosen as a camp site later than we had expected. Not too late, however, to enjoy the beauty of the woods and the sunset. We camped on the edge of a deep ravine in which we found a marvelous spring of clear, cold water. All about were great pine trees, and opposite the ravine a hillside of lovely aspen. We had a tent which attached to the car and as it looked like rain I put my bed inside while Timothy put his under a sheltering pine tree and tucked it about with a waterproof canvas.

After supper a caller appeared—a nice Navaho who informed me through Timothy that he greatly appreciated my interest in his people and was anxious to do all he could to help me. He told us that there were few people in that vicinity, most of them living on the other side of the aspen hill, and as it was impossible for us to get over there in the car he offered to lend us horses. I had no riding clothes with me but Timothy volunteered to get up early and drive back to the Trading Post to get me a pair of overalls.

Our friend had disappeared for a bit but returned shortly with a leg of mutton which I recognized as a gift of great worth and accepted with gratitude. He brought his two sons with him this time and we sat by the campfire smoking sociably and indulging our several fondnesses for watermelon—you doubtless remember the avidity of mine, and the Navahos are just as bad! Finally, when it began to rain, our party broke up and I went peacefully to bed in the shelter of the tent. From a sound sleep I was roused by a tugging at my tent, which was tied to the top of the car. It was Timothy pulling it down over my head in order to free the car and be off for my overalls! I had some difficulty in convincing him that it was only two o'clock, but finally a look at my watch sent him back to bed until five, when he was up and off.

It had rained quite hard in the night and with the tent down I found it was still sprinkling a little so I tucked the canvas well about my bed and snuggled in for a final nap. Waking again I sat up and looked around me. Certainly I seemed the only human atom in a primeval forest, but presently appeared a figure which, on approach, proved to be Jim Ferryboat, whose acquaintance I made last winter. Jim seemed pleased to see me, especially after he spied a melon in the near distance, and the fact that I sat in my nightgown in no wise disturbed him. He displayed an injured finger and brought my medicine bag to my bedside that I might dress it.

Learning that he was in quest of his horse I assured him that I thought it was "over there", and while he departed to see in the direction I pointed I hurried into my clothes. Jim returned horseless and accepted an invitation to breakfast. He made the fire and tended the coffee while I made pancakes and cooked the bacon. I do not know exactly what language Jim and I employed, as he does not speak English and I do not speak Navaho, but conversation did not languish as breakfast progressed. Jim consumed an entire pot of coffee except for the one cup I managed to extract for myself, and the pancakes disappeared as rapidly as I could get them cooked. Amongst other things, he informed me that I was fortunate not to have been visited during the night by a bear which prowled the neighborhood.

By and by Timothy arrived, starving. Another pot of coffee and a fresh supply of pancakes disappeared almost as rapidly as the first. Soon our steeds, a sorry Navaho horse and a burro, were brought to us. While I was retired behind the car getting into my overalls a number of Navahos wanting "aze" had gathered, and after supplying their wants Timothy and I set out on our rounds.

A busy morning followed, visiting summer hogans. These little shelters are, if possible, more primitive and less permanent than the winter hogans. They are usually built of a few supporting logs covered with green branches and are delightfully cool. When aspen branches are used the breezes touch the leaves to gentle whispering and the sunlight filtering through makes lovely shifting patterns on the floor. In one I saw the only constructed bed I have ever seen in a truly native hogan. It was a slightly elevated platform of slender aspen bolls placed together and heaped with fragrant fern fronds which abound in the region.

We returned to camp for a very late lunch, and just as we had gotten the fire started and put the leg of mutton to cook it began to pour and we were obliged to seek shelter in the car until the storm passed. By that time we were ravenous. When lunch was over the weather looked so uncertain that Timothy advised breaking camp without delay, and I appreciated his wisdom when we found the roads already badly washed and another heavy storm on the way.

We reached home late—tired, but satisfied that the trip had been worthwhile. We had ministered to twenty-two sick persons and have promised to repeat our visit next week if the weather permits. Can you bear to miss such escapades?

The summer shelter in the Cove, 1934

Red Rock
August 1, 1932

Dear Laura:

Your several letters begin to grow anxious in tone and I am really ashamed to have left them so long unanswered, but the summer is proving strenuous for me and time for letter writing simply doesn't exist.

The Field Nurse in a neighboring district, some ninety miles distant, is on vacation and when a rumor of a typhoid outbreak reached the hospital I was asked to make as frequent visits as possible to the neighborhood to check on suspected cases. This I have done three times a week and in addition have been having a clinic at the Trading Post, ninety miles away in another direction, once a week. With the prospect of nearly two hundred miles to travel over desert roads it behooves me to get an early start, so four mornings a week I am up and off as soon after seven as I can get Timothy started. We thump and bump over roads which you must experience before I try to describe them and risk an accusation which I should not relish. The sun blazes and no tree offers shade, the dust flies in smothering clouds, and we yet dread the coming of seasonal rains which either cause us to stick in mud or to wait for hours on the bank of a wash while the water goes down. It is disconcerting, to say the least, to find a sand creek which was as dry as dust on crossing in the morning, a raging torrent a few hours later. Timothy, trying to extricate the Chevvy from the 'dobe we sometime encounter, resembles nothing so much as a cat in paper shoes, and I am moved to mirth in spite of genuine distress over the necessity for his heroic efforts. The days between are crowded with visits to and from my own people and I am beginning to feel the strain in spite of a lively interest, and long for vacation time which will not come for another month.

Just here I was interrupted by one of my weaver friends who had brought a rug to show me. She came in so quietly on moccasined feet that I, busy typing, was not at first aware of her presence and I do not know how long she stood and interestedly watched me peg away. I gave her a cigarette and ash tray which she mistook for a cuspidor and used so frequently in that capacity that I was delighted to have thus saved my floor! After much sign conversation we had lunch, she partaking copiously of the coffee which I made for her special benefit. She took very kindly, too, to my rhubarb, of which she had four large servings, and of an entire loaf of bread there was nothing left. Her enjoyment was gratifying and her appreciation evident. She is Mrs. Hardbelly, grandmother of the baby with the burned hand who called me a fox. Mrs. Hardbelly calls me "Shedazy"—Little Sister.

Your Navaho friends and I are all eagerly looking forward to your long promised visit and we are planning all sorts of trips to the mountains for you. The Francises pay me frequent visits when they drive down from their mountain top summer home and nearly always they bring touching presents—sometimes a leg of lamb, sometimes a few new potatoes or other vegetables from their garden, and the other day Mrs. Francis brought an adorably cradled Navaho doll which she had made for me! I have promised to bring you picnicking to their mountain farm and I know you will love it. Francis has built a nice log house and the farm is flourishing. Mrs. Francis has her loom set up in the shade of a tree and weaves industriously when the spirit moves.

Red Rock
August 18, 1932

Dear Emily:

Yesterday morning an errand took me to the Trading Post and I was tempted, as always, to linger to watch and listen while the Trader did business with the Indians.

The Navahos seldom have money with which to buy the Trader's wares but trade on credit from their sheep, wool, pelts, blankets and silver. Their jewelry is generally pawned during the winter and redeemed in the spring when wool is sheared, or in the fall when their lambs are sold.

Trading, with the Navahos, is a serious matter not to be hastily done, and the Trader consequently has developed a matchless patience in dealing with them. I love to stand in a corner and watch the groups waiting to trade or stopping for gossip. In the winter time they gather around the stove in the center of the long store, in the summer find seats on the benches before the big windows. The affairs of the Reservation are here discussed and no trivial happening of local interest is overlooked or neglected. I have found no better way of getting news of patients than to let Timothy spend some time amongst the loiterers at the Post. I am always interested in the Indian's love of his jewelry and am happy with him when he redeems his pawn and swaggers amongst his fellows adorned with silver and turquoise rings and bracelets, handsome conchos and strings of wampum and coral. Our Trader is generously inclined to hold these prized possessions for them long after their pawn is legally "dead."

Next to the fascinating rows of pawned jewelry I love the rug room where stacks and stacks of "blankets" proclaim the industry of our weavers.

When I went home I was followed shortly by a young Medicine Man who, though quite reserved and rather shy, has shown decided symptoms of friendliness. He spent hours in my rooms, evidently interested in many of my possessions, had lunch with me and finally disclosed the purpose of his visit. He told Timothy that he recognized my interest in his sings and ceremonies and wished to invite me to see a sand painting he was to do the following Sunday for a patient who lived about forty miles away.

Endeavoring to emulate the politeness which is so marked a characteristic of the Navaho, I accepted the invitation, and Sunday morning accordingly found us traversing a bumpy road to the distant

Red Rock Trading Post, 1932

hogan. There we were cordially received by my friend and his brother Medicine Man and taken into the hogan to see the sand painting which had just been completed. To my surprise an old man pointed out various figures for us, explaining their identity and significance. When the ceremony was about to begin, the patient, to whom I was a stranger, obviously objected to my presence, so hastily expressing my admiration for the sand painting I departed. My friend followed me from the hogan with an invitation to return to subsequent paintings, of which there were to be three in this series.

On the third day I returned, and this time I went armed with my medicine bag, in response to a request on my last visit, and was amused to find myself holding a small clinic outside the hogan for Medicine Men, patient and guests. The Medicine Men frequently stop at my dispensary on their way to or from sings to ask for "khosaze" (cough medicine), and when one hears them sing for days and nights on end the reason is readily understood—a soothing throat remedy must be very welcome.

In visiting hogans I am invariably impressed by the happy home life I find therein. Except where there is extreme illness, entire families gather to enjoy visitors, and laughter and good natured joking are much enjoyed. The children, though usually shy, seldom cry and always submit to necessary treatment much more readily than most of the small white patients I have known, and once they decide to make friends they do so in whole-hearted fashion. Their affection for one another is evidenced in many ways and the feeling between parents and children is as obvious and tender as I have ever seen. I am, of course, interested in the amicability existing between the several wives and families of the older men. These wives are not infrequently sisters, and never but once or twice have I found evidence of jealousy between them. Usually each wife has her own hogan, though I have seen two living in the same hogan at times.

As in other communities the world over, there occurs an occasional family row, usually precipitated by jealousy between husband and wife, but the atmosphere of the home is generally good natured and happy and dominated by characteristic Navaho politeness.

Red Rock
October 2, 1932

Dear Marion:

Just back from a delightful vacation spent partly in Colorado Springs with Laura and partly with Emily in Nebraska. I am sufficiently rested and refreshed to consider the renewal of a lagging correspondence! I am sure I deserve your reproachful card, but busy days precluded letter writing and an occasional hot evening at home was hardly to be spent close to a kerosene lamp.

Shortly before my vacation began Laura came down for another of her brief visits and the days were crowded with happy happenings. I wished for you particularly on one of our weekly camp clinics in the mountains, where I go to be within reach of the Navahos who are spending the summer there with their sheep. We had made our camp in the usual spot and had wandered into a lovely meadow where we unexpectedly discovered mushrooms of an edible variety. We spent some time gathering enough to serve with a steak which was awaiting cooking in the camp and then stopped for a bit to enjoy the secluded beauty of our surroundings. Turning suddenly in a new direction I saw a solitary figure standing in the edge of the wood watching us in silence. After staying motionless for awhile he seemed to accept us as friends and approached with a shy smile and a diffident welcome.

We indulged in a bit of friendly discourse, which could scarcely be called conversation although he quickly understood and accepted our invitation to lunch and returned with us to camp where we had Timothy to interpret for us. From an odd package he wore slung on his hip I had suspected that he was a Medicine Man, and observing my interest in the pack he told Timothy that though he would not ordinarily show his medicine to strangers he would be glad to show it to me since our professions were the same and he appreciated my efforts to help his people. Thereupon he reverently untied the buckskin wrappings and disclosed the oddest assortment of objects imaginable. There were the skulls of two long-billed birds (Laura thinks they were two big blue heron) attached to two sticks which were covered and trimmed with eagle feathers and colored strings, tiny arrow heads, and bits of colored shell; several prayer sticks similarly trimmed, and an ancient turtle shell, which he used as a medicine cup. There were numerous small buckskin bags filled with medicine, and a rattle made of polished deer hoofs, hung to a

Setah Begay, Navaho medicine man, 1932

handle by buckskin thongs. He told us that the pack was very old, he having purchased it in his youth from an old, old Medicine Man who had had it all his life. The purchase price had been thirty sheep and an equal number of blankets. After lunch, which he evidently enjoyed though he thought our steak insufficiently cooked and both he and Timothy refused our mushrooms, it began to rain and we foregathered in the tent where I whiled away the time by making Timothy translate for him my own dimly remembered version of Medusa and the Gorgon's head. This he thought a grand story and said it reminded him of some of the old Navaho legends, which he was about to recount while we sat breathless, but alack, a sound of thunder warned him that these tales must not be told until the thunder had gone to sleep, and we were obliged to be satisfied with his promise to spend several days with me next winter, since he says his stories cannot be told in a day! He was distressed over the fact that his turtle shell medicine cup is cracked and leaks, and I have secured another one for him and hope for an early opportunity to present it.

Homeward bound next day we stopped just at the foot of the mountains to pay a hogan visit to a patient and were enchanted by the scene we came upon. This family had just harvested its wheat crop and the boys, mounted on horses, were merrily trotting around on a heap of golden straw, threshing the grain in primitive Navaho fashion. At one side lay a mound of winnowed wheat, with the crude implements used in the process close at hand. The colorful costumes of the women and children gathered on the edge of the circle, the setting sun touching the yellow straw to golden glory in the foreground and the sky to a gorgeous curtain beyond, made a picture which Laura's camera couldn't resist, and I have another entry in my Navaho memories.

Red Rock
November 13, 1932

Dear Emily:

Ever since my vacation I have been hearing rumors of a Fire Dance to be held at Lukachukai but it has seemed impossible to get a definite date. I was eager to see it, of course, and when I wrote Laura about it she dropped business at home and came down late in October, when I thought it would surely transpire. I was chagrinned on her arrival to have to admit that definite information as to the date was still lacking, but I was delighted to have a sympathetic companion during the closing days of the Presidential campaign as I got it over my radio. Exciting days surely.

The Fire Dance is the culmination of the nine-day Mountain Chant, and while the whole ceremony must be absorbingly interesting, we were obliged to be content to see the spectacular end. Even to the last we were unable to get very definite information and were still uncertain as to whether the final dance was to take place on Wednesday or Thursday night following the election. In order to be certain of seeing it we decided to go over Wednesday afternoon, taking camp equipment, determined to stay over two nights if necessary—and did.

When the news spread that we were going, friends began to besiege us with requests for a ride and we decided we would have to take both Laura's car and mine. There were Francis and Mrs. Francis, Mary and her little boy, Jack, Bushy Head, Laura, Timothy, and me, besides tent, beds, camping equipment, and food.

We were too late to see the final sand painting, but preparation and practice for Thursday night were in full swing. It was a scene of busy interest. A large ceremonial hogan had been erected on the desert some distance from the handsome vermilion cliffs skirting the mountains. The cliffs, when we arrived, were touched into splendor by the setting sun, and with the abundant gray-green sage brush dotted with vivid touches of color in Navaho costume, made a picture which will be long in fading from our memory. As night came on a strong wind, with an uncomfortable accompaniment of sand, sprang up and the Navahos took refuge in a brush corral where a comfortable fire was burning. There, during practice, one of their leaders stepped to the middle of the setting, clapped for silence and delivered a long harangue which to us was unintelligible. The interest was evident and we were curious. Out of the midst of Navaho suddenly sounded a name which thrilled us: "Roosevelt." "Washington" and "Hoover" followed. Thus at midnight beneath the stars, in the depths of the Navaho desert, we received the election returns. After that the dances for the following night were rehearsed over and over again. We watched until the wind, sand, cold and smoke drove us to our tents for shelter, and for long after we were wrapped in our blankets we lay and listened to the sound of Indian voices in songs they rehearsed for the culminating fire dances.

Next day, though the wind and sand continued to blow, no chance was afforded for flagging interest. Busy commotion was stirring on every hand. Here was a large temporary shelter used as cook house, with several fires surrounded by experts at work preparing Navaho delicacies for the coming feast. As we stood watching we were invited to try our hands at working and moulding wads from huge dishpans of dough into the proper shape for cooking on hot stones in flat cakes. Our efforts occasioned the greatest amusement, and good natured laughter at our expense filled the enclosure.

In a sheltered depression was a group practicing again the night's song and dance. Beyond the ceremonial hogan a great stack of firewood was growing to incredible size, though we were assured much more was needed to supply the night's demand. From every direction came men bringing in cut trees for the erection later of the huge corral which was to surround the audience and participants in the night-long ceremony. Now and again when we encountered familiar faces from across the mountain our hearts were warmed by the pleasure evidenced in the meeting and we began to feel ourselves happily amongst friends.

Just at sunset a group of singers, led by the chief Medicine Man, emerged from the ceremonial hogan. Then began the ceremony of dedication. The Medicine Man carried a basket of sacred meal and, followed by the singers with voice and rattle, he sprinkled the meal in a great circle (possibly 200 feet or more in diameter). Around this circle the waiting Navahos dragged and placed the trees they had been bringing in all day, making a green corral some six or eight feet high, opening to the east. A tremendous pile of wood was placed in the center ready for the great fire and then we all began to move in, bag and baggage.

Though the gathered crowd was great and eager there was no pushing, no crowding or jostling, no rude seeking of preferential seats. Minding our own manners we chose places at a modest distance from the front and seated ourselves on the ground behind tall and blanket-wrapped figures. Being short of stature we were busily craning our necks for better vision when we were surprised and delighted to be beckoned to the front row by one of the Masters of Ceremony. This unexpected and pleasing courtesy must surely be due to the regard in which Timothy is held by his people.

All around the circle the audience grouped, with many smaller fires in their midst for warmth and for the cooking of meals which went on more or less all night while the dance was in progress. While the crowd was gathering and arranging itself we could hear the Medicine Men chanting and shaking their rattles in the ceremonial hogan nearby, and finally at the sound of a whistle a dozen Navahos in breech clouts, with bodies painted white, came running in and danced around the great central fire, which by this time was roaring and throwing out tremendous heat. They carried sticks with tufts of eagle feathers on the end and these they thrust in to flames until the feathers were burned off. Then singing a song, which Timothy told me called the blackened feathers to "come white again," they shook the sticks, and lo, a bunch of new feathers appeared. This miracle was thoroughly enjoyed by the audience and I could get none to admit that he knew how it was accomplished. The feather dance was another piece of unexplained magic. A large eagle feather lying in a flat basket erected itself and danced in time with a little girl who danced before it. Then a man took a mass of burning,dripping pitch from the fire and dropped it over the hands of another who remained unburned while the audience gasped in wonder. Throughout the night dance succeeded dance, each dancing team preceded and accompanied by a group of singers with rattles, and each dance was perfectly timed to follow the last so that the night's performance ran smoothly and without pause.

Despite our warmest clothes and the enwrapping blankets we had brought, despite the roaring and leaping of flames from the great fire we faced, Laura and I grew desperately cold and marveled at the apparent comfort of our neighbors. Our appetites were not whetted by the odor of boiling mutton and cheap coffee which surrounded us and mingled with the heavy smoke issuing from many fires, but never was I more touched than when my friend Mrs. Hardbelly, noting our lack of food and evidently recalling the occasions when I had shared my lunch with her, touched my shoulder and insisted on giving us of her fare.

And so we sat through the long night watching the strangely costumed figures as they danced in the brilliant glow of the mighty fire, seeming at times to our shivering selves to be absorbed in worship of the god of

Navahos by firelight, 1933

warmth and life. The encircling audience of more than 1000 Indians (in which were two white faces besides our own) sat absorbed in the beauty before them, totally unaware of the part they played in the magnificent spectacle we enjoyed. The whole night through we heard no noisy laughter, saw no slightest sign of drinking or ribaldry, and finally agreed that we had never before been part of a more delightful throng.

Just before dawn the first twelve dancers reappeared. With them was a Medicine Man who lighted four cedar torches which were seized by one of the dancers who ran yelling around the circle, whirling and tossing a blazing torch over the heads of the audience in each of the four directions. Then each dancer was given a torch which he lighted at the fire and began a wild dance 'round the fire, each beating his own and his neighbors' bodies with his burning torch. It was amazingly spectacular and exciting and a grand climax to a marvelous night.

With the rising of the sun the corral was opened in the three unbroken directions and the crowd made orderly exit.

Red Rock
November 15, 1932

Dear Helen:

Laura has promised to tell you all about the Fire Dance, which I am sure you would have enjoyed as we did, and as there have been no other activities of interest in our neighborhood of late, that leaves me without much subject matter for a letter! Perhaps, however, you may be interested in the antics of the Chevvy with the coming of cold weather.

When we got back from the Fire Dance early Friday morning we found a boy waiting with a message asking me to see an old man who lives about fifteen miles from here. I set out at once and found the man badly in need of hospitalization, though unwilling (as is usual) to go, since acute pain to which he is subject had subsided for a time. Argument and persuasion, reason, logic and warning are alike unavailing with the Navahos in the matter of illness (which they always think is due to the influence of chindis or evil spirits), so after doing what I could and explaining what relief he might expect from hospital treatment, I left with the assurance I would take him in to the hospital any time he decided to go. Various other cases kept me busy until about eleven o'clock that night, when I tumbled into bed fairly drunk with sleep. At two a.m. I roused with difficulty to answer a rap, and here again was the boy, unable to talk but signifying that father was ready now to go to the hospital. I sent him for Timothy while I dressed, and then as Timothy failed to appear I got the car and went over to his house. Poor little Timothy, making up lost sleep, had gotten up when the boy called, put on his shirt wrong side out in the dark, and then discouraged and cold had crawled into his warm blankets for a moment's comfort and was lost hopelessly in slumber! I took him over some coffee which I had put on my stove, and we were off. Picking up the old man we had gained the road once more when the car sputtered and stopped. Timothy's coaxing and admonishing were useless. He tried all his usual tricks, to no avail, and he was even unable to diagnose the trouble. It was obvious lack of gas there in the engine tho there was plenty in the tank. It must therefore be in the "feed," but Timothy could blow through the disconnected tube with ease. "So," said I, with logic, "the stoppage is in the tank." We tried poking a wire in and found a tube leading toward the bottom and were finally obliged to take the tank off and empty its contents (fortunately we had an empty five gallon can with us) to find it was clogged with ice. Some gas tank! Relieved of the ice, with its gas returned to the tank and tank and pipes connected again, the Chevvy started briskly and we reached the hospital about nine a.m.

Timothy Kellywood, 1932

Red Rock
December 15, 1932

Dear Laura:

It seems long since I have heard from you and is doubtless as long since I have written. I am still surprised at the fullness of my days and at the rapidity of their passage, and am appalled when I realize that Christmas is at hand and no preparations made! You know that I have determined to confine my Christmas giving almost entirely to some few Navaho friends this year, and my heart aches when I realize how pitifully few I may include in my small festivities. The prospect of a Mission party such as last year's is small. I gather that funds are nil and the Missionary is planning to spend Christmas with his wife, who, you know, is away.

I am planning a dinner for twelve, a tree for about twenty, and had expected to go to Gallup this week to do the necessary shopping, but last weekend it began to snow and blow and has kept at it almost constantly since, so that the road is probably as difficult or more difficult (if possible!) than it was last year. No one has ventured to use a car so far and I am beginning to wonder if we are not really snowbound. If it proves truly so I shall have to send Timothy rabbit hunting for our Christmas dinner and depend upon the Trading Post stock and my needle for gifts.

If opportunity for mailing this presents itself I shall send at the same time a parcel with a gift for you (a souvenir of the locality), and a white goatskin rug which I shall ask you to deliver to Martha for me. I am avoiding many packages in order to simplify mailing, since I am uncertain how it may be done. I have recently discovered the possibility of getting these lovely long haired goat skins and think they will make nice bedside rugs for cold weather.

Have I told you that the Francises, who have five boys of their own, have recently adopted a little girl? She is a cunning thing, between three and four years old I should judge, and has been abandoned by her own parents. Mrs. Francis and I have dressed her in a little red velvet blouse and a long blue skirt made from a dress of mine, and she is a picture. With better food than she has been accustomed to, and affectionate care which she has probably never known before, she is blossoming like a small flower and I find her as entrancing as any little child I have ever known. I am making a Navaho doll for her Christmas gift, dressed in a copy of her own new clothes.

It is an utterly different world we look upon these days—all white, dark blue and gray. Today the mountains, partly visible for the first time in a week, are deeply blue, the sky a soft gray (seeming to promise more snow!) and the earth a vast expanse of purest white. Since the snowfall Grant and Timothy have been out on frequent hunting expeditions. To date they have shot nothing, but the fun is good.

The Trader has just sent word that he will make an effort to reach Shiprock early tomorrow morning. This goes with him, and in case it is my last message before Christmas it is as full of loving Christmas wishes as a letter may be.

Red Rock
December 26, 1932

Dear Laura:

Where and how shall I begin to say all the things which are crowding to be said? First, I must say thank you, and thank you, and thank you—so many, many times—for my birthday gift, my Christmas gift, and for the more than wonderful box for my tree and party. Every smallest thing was just right and has afforded more pleasure and joy to us all than you can ever know. Just a week before Christmas we made a desperate effort and got to Gallup. It was a hard trip—twenty-five miles to the highway and then 100 miles of icy road to Gallup. We had a dense fog all the way which froze to the windshield both inside and out and made driving the road terribly difficult for poor Timothy. The thermometer was below zero and we were none too warm. Despite a very early start and every effort for haste we got home at midnight. Timothy made a roaring fire and we had hot chocolate, toast and apple sauce and gloated over our packages until I sent him home at one-thirty.

I had spent my last cent, but never felt richer in my life! There were heaped on my bed, blankets for Mrs. Francis and the Ute Woman; a nice comfort for Ethel, who boasts a bed; sweater coat, warm gloves and leather puttees for Timothy; a drip coffee pot and a pound of good coffee for Grant, who loves mine; half a dozen pretty cups and saucers for Lilly; material for a gay red skirt with black and yellow trimming for Mary; gloves for Francis and Woody; caps and gloves for the Francis boys; and toys and toys for the other children, with an extra supply for unexpecteds—and tree trimmings!

The following Thursday we ventured out again and succeeded in reaching Farmington, where we got a huge turkey and all the necessities for our Christmas feast, besides candy, apples, and oranges for the tree.

On the way home we found your marvelous boxes, with similar ones from Emily and the Eyres, and a most unexpected surprise from Mr. Postlethwaite! He sent two splendid suits which are just right for Timothy and Woody, who are both in rags, a dozen boxes of candy and a carton of cigarettes. Timothy and I felt like two Santa Clauses. But our road is so terrible—almost its entire length so deeply drifted that it is impossible to find—that Timothy and I are determined not to venture out again this winter! Timothy thinks it a pity we didn't fold the road up and put it away before the snow came. Certainly it is of no use to anybody as it is.

With such a wealth of gifts on hand Timothy could scarcely wait for Christmas Day, but I determinedly refused to let him trim the tree until Christmas Eve. We had to put it in my dispensary room and I knew it would offer temptations for more Navahos than I could possibly accommodate.

Christmas morning I had breakfast with the Trader family and came home about eleven to start preparations for the day. I had invited my dinner guests for a six o'clock dinner. Francis had brought me a big squash for pumpkin pies for the feast and Ethel came over to help prepare the meal. Neither she nor I had ever made pies, but we were struggling valiantly with them and the turkey when to my consternation my guests began to arrive at one-thirty! I could not send them down to the dispensary as the tree was a surprise to come later, so I had to crowd them into my sitting room and, of course, the children constantly overflowed into the kitchen and under foot so that the rest of the afternoon was a trifle hectic. As soon as the turkey was done we repaired to the dispensary for dinner. In true Navajo fashion, sitting on rugs on the floor, we consumed dish pans full of slaw, mashed potatoes and cranberry sauce, platters and platters of bread, my coffee pot three times full of coffee, and the entire turkey. Squash pie completed the repast, and I am sure I was the only one present who wasn't filled to the brim. My duties as hostess left scant time for eating.

As soon as it was dark, came Grant and his family with numerous unexpected relatives, the Trader's family, George Begay and his family, Timothy's uncle unexpectedly released from jail for the party, Lee and his family. All told there were more than forty, instead of the twenty invited guests. Fortunately I had anticipated something of the sort and the Trader had let me have a supply of warm gloves and stockings—to be returned if not needed. These, with the generous unexpected boxes I have mentioned, saved the day and nobody was slighted.

As I stood beside our lighted tree with the lamp extinguished and looked around I wished for you and your camera to catch and keep for me the eager, dusky faces raised in the candle light and alight themselves with happy pleasure in the gifts, candy and fruit Timothy and I were dispensing. The children with their toys were delightful to watch. The little Francis girl was especially touching with her doll and a cheap little red wagon. Nothing else and nobody existed for her the rest of the evening. Charles was a picture in Elizabeth's little outgrown red zipper suit, and Albert looked like our adopted puppy toddling around.[13]

Later we played "Spin the Plate" and "Who Has the Button," the only two games I could think of that were simple enough for our conglomerate ages and tongues.

When my guests were gone and I went tiredly to bed it was with the satisfying reflection that I had never before had so happily successful a party.

13. Charles and Albert were the sons of Timothy Kellywood. Elizabeth was the daughter of Forster's sister Emily.

Red Rock
January 3, 1933

Dear Helen:

   Do you remember the lovely drive we took to Red Mexican's home over near the red cliffs? The old man has been quite sick with Flu and I have made several very difficult trips to his place through the snow to consult and collaborate with the Medicine Man who has been singing for him. I was greatly surprised to find him to be the man we met in the mountains last summer, whom I have not seen since until now. I was delighted to find him cordial and evidently glad to have me work with him. He held up both hands with fingers folded, except the two forefingers which he placed side by side to show how we would work together. I sat and watched him as he sang and the earnest kindness of the face with its closed eyes and serious expression was impressive, and the monotonous clink of his deer hoof rattle soothing, so that I couldn't wonder much at Red Mexican's evident faith in his power.

   I grew anxious about Red Mexican as symptoms developed which suggested mastoid infection, and when I felt that I was sufficiently well established in the good graces of both Medicine Man and patient I described to them as well as I could the operation necessary to relieve the pain he was suffering. To my delight he sent a message last clinic day that he was willing to go to the hospital. Timothy took the car and went for him while the doctor and I had lunch, but as time passed and no Timothy or patient appeared we set out as search party and dragged them out of a drift! This week the doctor reports Red Mexican recovering finely from the operation.

   Travel this winter is proving even more difficult than it was last, so that I dread any call to visit hogans or the necessity of a trip to town. The weather has been so desperately cold that the snow has had no chance to melt and the wind has blown so persistently that we never know where we will encounter new drifts. Last week coming back from Shiprock we stuck in a drift and in attempting to pull out broke the universal joint of the Chevvy. While poor Timothy and Woody walked thirteen miles for help I sat in the car and kept as warm as possible on a zero night. About midnight I was cheered to see lights approaching. It was Timothy and Woody in a borrowed car, but the two weary boys had to take the chains from my tires and transfer them to the others before we could start for home. It was two a.m. before we got in and made a fire to thaw us out.

Fortunately I had made some delicious mushroom soup before I went in that morning and it was quickly warmed. Food, heat and rest were delightfully welcome and comforting. The boys were tired and sore as to muscles but seemed all right next day. Timothy went back and had my car hauled in to the garage and brought it back in good shape Sunday. I tremble to get the bill.

Red Rock
January 10, 1933

Dear Marion:

Your very nice and very welcome letter deserves a prompt reply and I am tempted to try to share with you an experience I have had lately which seems to me almost more interesting than any I have had before.

News reached me the other day of the illness of old Navaho Jim, a respected member of our community, of whom I am quite fond and whose family I have always found friendly and responsive to my advances. This time, however, I was doubtful of a welcome after I heard that the Missionary had preceded me in an effort to break up the "sing" the old man was having and wanted to take him to the hospital. Dubious but hopeful I determined to risk a visit and went armed with a few simple remedies and comforts which I guessed might be appropriate.

To my surprise I was greeted quite cordially outside by the old man's wife, but I waited while Timothy went into the hogan, where the Medicine Man was singing, to ask if I might enter. He returned with permission and I went in. As I entered some one made a remark which was greeted with laughter. I knew, of course, that it was at my expense, but it sounded good natured and I was sure it was not offensive. Timothy told me afterwards that the remark had been "Oh, this is one of our own medicine men, so it is all right." The idea that I am a medicine man and at their service is a source of kindly amusement to them always.

I stayed a short time and was invited to return that night for a devil chasing ceremony, which was deemed necessary to rid Jim of chindi influence, which he had incurred by work in the Mesa Verde ruins last summer. Back I went about six o'clock with a sack of sugar, some coffee and cigarettes, to insure my welcome. It is always customary for friends and relatives to contribute in this manner to the refreshment offered by a patient's family when a sing is in progress. The old wife took me in charge and at the proper moment I was led into the hogan where the ceremony was about to begin.

It was an unusually large and spacious hogan, and opposite the door beyond the fire sat the Medicine Man, whom I was surprised to recognize as Grant's father, with the patient seated on his left, Mrs. Jim took her place on her husband's left, I at her left, and other women, as they appeared, at my left. The gentlemen sat across the hogan to the right of the Medicine Man. The flame and glow from the fire in the center of the hogan furnished the only light. When some thirty or forty of us were finally gathered the Medicine Man and his assistants shook their rattles (gourds containing pieces of shell) and began to sing. Navaho Jim thereupon removed shirt and trousers and sat, a rather pathetic figure, in a gee string. When, however, at a signal from the Medicine Man, he rose, he presented a magnificently tall and beautifully tapering figure, and it was only when in circling the hogan he stepped into the stronger light of the fire one saw that his muscles were beginning to betray age.

He came to a stand beside the Medicine Man, who continued to sing while his assistant shook his rattle, and then the audience took up the song—for so it is called, this weird monotonous utterance which to my ear has no melody and strange rhythm. Meanwhile the Medicine Man was performing certain rites upon Jim's body with sprays of yucca and bunches of some weed which his assistants had prepared. This procedure occurred twice, including the circling of the hogan by Jim, and then two youths disrobed and after rubbing their bodies with ashes stood before the Medicine Man who decorated them with necklaces and bracelets of arrowheads and crowns of eagle feathers. Then with bunches of eagle feathers in their hands they proceeded to brush the devils from the patient and chased them from the hogan, uttering meanwhile strange animal-like cries. Following the devils through the door they could be heard circling the hogan outside with the same weird cries. On reentering they were given a gourd filled with some fluid, with which they annointed their bodies, and finally resumed their clothing and the ceremony was ended.

I long for the descriptive ability to show you the thing as I saw it—the cupping dome of the hogan with the fire glowing in the center, the group of blanketed figures seated on sheepskins close to the encircling wall, the dark faces which gleamed and faded as the fire flame leaped and died, the lovely softly colored figures of the two boys and the old man, and the ancient Medicine Man whose toothless face, framed in straggling hair and crowned by a band of bright red rag, smiled at me across the fire. And once when the firelight waned I looked up and saw through the opening in the top of the hogan the only familiar sight of that night—a bit of velvety sky agleam with golden stars.

Navaho Jim's Hogan, 1932

Red Rock
January 30, 1933

Dear Emily,

One of the pitiful phases of reservation life which strikes me as particularly hard is that of the "returned students." These boys and girls have spent a varying number of years in boarding schools where they have learned to live by standards impossible to hogan life, have been taught to regard their fathers' religion as superstition, failing meanwhile to grasp the meaning of Christianity, have apparently small chance and less incentive to make use of the education thus acquired, and so present a picture of idle, useless youth.

It is, however, a picture surprisingly good natured and unvicious, which makes one dream impossible dreams of a social experiment needing only fairly ample funds and workers of sufficiently elastic imagination and sympathy, insight and understanding to make use of the splendid heritage and tradition which belong to these people, helping them to adapt to their simple needs aids and comforts civilization has made possible to us.

To my observation, the girls seem to return more adaptably to hogan life than do the boys. Back in Navaho costume they often pretend not to understand English and are in no way to be distinguished from their sisters who have never been to school.

The boys, on the other hand, hang about the Trading Post and frequent any gathering which offers entertainment, seeming particularly eager for opportunities to practice the sports they learned to love at school.

Last fall I used to take a team to Shiprock to play basketball, and in a particularly sympathetic moment I promised Timothy that if he and his basketball team practiced seriously I would take them to Colorado Springs for a game. All winter, in spite of hardships and handicaps occasioned by bad weather and roads, they have worked faithfully and hard, and I was able to secure a date for them with the Fountain Valley School team in Colorado Springs, coinciding with, or rather just following a meeting I meant to attend in Santa Fe. Great was the excitement when my intention was announced.

It was a hurriedly arranged affair at the last, since the date of the meeting (January 19th) was not certainly known to us until a trip to the Post Office January 17th. This meant we must be off next morning and we hurried home to begin preparations, picking up on the road a woman whom I had taken to the hospital not long ago for treatment. She was homeward bound, and as we were unable to reach her hogan in the snow and she was not anxious to walk home in the dark, I allowed her to sleep in my dispensary.

Our start was delayed by a bad snow and wind storm, but taking advantage of the first lull we set out some time during the forenoon. Halfway to the highway we came upon a stranded car in which a Navaho family had been marooned for hours. They hailed us as rescuers and we crowded the man, woman and child into the places three of our team were to fill in Shiprock. The hoodoo seemed thereupon to transfer itself from the Navahos' car to ours and trouble began somewhere in the feed system. By dint of his native wiles and witchery, Timothy got us into Shiprock about eight o'clock that night, too late to have anything done to the car. Next day it was in the shop until afternoon, when at last we set forth on our journey, too late to make the Santa Fe meeting but with the excitement of Colorado Springs ahead.

These boys (except Timothy, who had had a trip to Santa Fe and one to Colorado Springs with me) had never been further than Gallup or neighboring Indian schools, and their delight in the trip, their good sportsmanship and their gentlemanly behaviour throughout made it well worth the effort and expense to me.

We were in Colorado Springs four days, they played four games—won two, lost two—and had a marvelous time. Colorado Springs school teams were all anxious to play my Indians, and it was hard to tear ourselves away.

Red Rock
January 30, 1932

Dear Laura:

Though you will remember that when I left Colorado Springs with my basketball team a storm threatened, we were half way between Pueblo and Walsenburg before it really inconvenienced us. Then we found ourselves on the outskirts of such a sand storm as I had never before witnessed. It was impossible to see objects two feet ahead and cars were lined up by the dozens waiting for a lull.

After waiting about six hours, Timothy thought it was not quite so thick and started into it. I admit I was scared to death, particularly when our engine stalled and refused to start again. Other cars were in the same predicament all around us, and though we were sure it was sand in the feed tubes it was impossible to clean anything, with sand still blowing in steady sheets.

Soon the road crew came along and offered to tow us back to Greenhorn on the outskirts of the storm. When we got there we found the one garage full of cars being worked on, but by then the wind had lulled and Timothy managed outside to clean out the sand and we were able to start once more—a very tired, hungry and gritty party.

Never in my life have I known anything as difficult to stand pleasantly as the chewing and vociferous popping which had been going on in my close shut car all day. Please find out who contributed the gum and kill him outright and in cold blood!

In Walsenburg at last—fresh air and food were welcome as never before and I was ready for bed early, but my Navahos sallied forth to explore Walsenburg. According to next morning's report, they located a basketball game but were unable to persuade the winning team to take them on.

That day we lunched late in Santa Fe, paid a visit to the Laboratory of Anthropology and then went on to Albuquerque, where the boys spent the night at the Indian school.

Next day we were beginning to feel the end of our eventful journey near when we had a puncture, and, before we could have it repaired, a blowout. Timothy patched the punctured tube but when it was ready to be pumped up it wouldn't pump and must come off again and be patched in four more places!

We were cheered by a warm welcome from the Trader's family. We had locked the cat in the house so securely that the Trader had had to take the door off the hinges to get him out. He then disappeared but came rushing in today ravenously welcoming. Little Danny dog was here to greet me and so happy over my return that I almost wept.

Poor Timothy's eyes suffered cruelly in the sand storm the other day and this morning we discovered a tiny ulcer on the edge of the iris. The doctor was here today for clinic and has ordered treatment which is very painful and we are both suffering—Timothy who endures the pain and I who must inflict it.

The doctor brought several of my patients home from the hospital, among them Flora and a nice new baby. She had a very difficult time and the doctor says she would surely have lost her baby and probably her own life without the facilities and care afforded by the hospital.

Red Rock
February 23, 1933

Dear Laura:

None could say that this Navaho desert life lacks incident and excitement! Late yesterday afternoon, as I was beginning to think longingly of bed after a day spent suffering from a feverish head cold while interviewing forty patients, Francis came in.

He sat for what seemed hours discussing trivialities before he inquired if I meant to go to Shiprock Saturday. I replied that I did not know, and then in characteristic Navaho fashion, after all this preamble, he disclosed the real purpose of his visit. Timothy was wanted at a Navajo trial Saturday! "What has Timothy been up to?" I asked. "Rape," says Francis, bold as brass. It seems that a woman, a patient who spent the night in my dispensary the night before we left for our trip to Colorado Springs, had accused Timothy of attacking her.

Sick anyhow, I spent a far from happy night, and this morning broke the news to Timothy. The boy was evidently amazed and emphatically denied the charge. He was all for going at once to see the woman and set out to borrow a horse from Francis. Francis was not at home but Mrs. Francis dissuaded him from going alone. Later when Francis returned he discouraged Timothy's going at all and promises to talk to the woman tomorrow himself.

The situation is serious certainly, but I am nevertheless moved to occasional secret mirth by the air of tragic excitement in which we move. Everybody is anxious to discuss the matter with me and the discussion is very frank, very broad. Francis is rather sophisticated and very detailed; Timothy naive, outspoken and picturesquely descriptive. I am more deeply interested and concerned than I ever expected to be in such a situation. Timothy tells me not to worry, that as long as the accusation is untrue we have no need to worry, but in spite of his brave words I can see that he is troubled—his sensitive mouth is very expressive.

I will let you know the result of the trial later.

Red Rock
March 2, 1933

Dear Laura:

Hectic and harrowing days! Little sleep and less digestion for several days and nights, due partly to my concern over Timothy's plight and partly to a sinus infection following a bad cold.

I took Timothy in to Shiprock on Friday to ask the Agent to come out on Saturday to insure a fair trial. He came, but testimony was against Timothy and he is sentenced to thirty days in jail. Timothy continues to protest his innocence and says (I think truly) that the witnesses against him all want his job. George Begay had the nerve to come to me before the trial was fairly over to ask for it. I shook my finger in his face and said "Don't you dare ask me for Timothy's job!" George's eyes got big and bigger and he backed out of the door murmuring a faint "Yes, Ma'am."

While I am in a way ashamed of my lack of control, I cannot altogether regret this outburst since I am convinced it has saved me the aggravation of other applicants!

Everyone hereabouts believes Timothy guilty because they maintain that the Navahos are all "like that," and with what looks like reason on one side and my fondness for and faith in Timothy on the other, I have been cruelly torn. Finally, however, reason, too, has stepped to Timothy's side as I recall the accusations made against him after each of his trips abroad with me and remember how he disproved each, and my own conclusion that his friends were jealous. This, I am convinced, is a frame-up, and Timothy's job is his again when his sentence is served. He has arranged that Woody shall fill his place and support his family during his absence. Woody can interpret for me, act as guide, and dig me out if I stick in the mess of mud that is now our road.

This jail business is one of the most amusing travesties I have encountered in this funny world. The jail is a small log house in Shiprock where prisoners are lodged and fed. They seem at liberty to roam at will, and upon request obtain leave to visit their families for days at a time, provided they return on the day appointed. After two days therein, Timothy opined to me that now he would grow fat, his only discomfort being occasioned by bed bugs whose bites he bitterly resents.

After several days' incarceration Timothy was, to our surprise, sent out here to serve the rest of his term helping carpenters and plasterers who are getting this building ready for a day school. The Government under the new Indian Service Program is establishing day schools throughout the reservation supplementing the boarding schools which are inadequate and often unacceptable to the Indians, and the building in which I am housed has been leased for the purpose.

Red Rock
April 4, 1933

Dear Emily:

Poor old Navaho Jim has been sick off and on all winter. When I offer to take him to the hospital he shakes his head and tells Timothy to tell me, "If it is my time to die I wish to die amongst my own people, not amongst strangers whose words and ways I cannot understand," and I know that under like circumstances I should feel as he does and refrain from urging.

When the doctor comes for clinic he usually goes out with me to Jim's hogan and prescribes for his comfort at least. I contribute an occasional gift of fruit, which the old man loves, and it is amusing that he pretends to attribute any benefit which follows to the fruit rather than to the medicine. The other day he told me that the big orange (grapefruit) I had left last time had cured him, though his improvement was not apparent to me.

He has impoverished himself by having sing after sing, so that one misses the signs of affluence which formerly adorned his person and his wife—the strings of coral and wampum, the turquoise and silver jewelry, and the silver buttons which they love, have all been pawned to furnish food for the countless guests these ceremonies have attracted. The medicine men have taken fee from sheep and goats of a fast diminishing flock.

Just recently he has had what is usually called a Squaw Dance, though it is truly the present day adaptation of what was the Scalp Dance of days gone by. This ceremony is accomplished in four stages, the beginning and the ending scenes being enacted at the patient's hogan, the two intermediate ones at a distance. I was able only to see the first and last stages and was sorry to miss altogether the dances which filled several days with revelry.

Preparations had been going on for several days when one morning I was invited to see the trimming of the rattle stick. When I entered the hogan I found Jim seated near the Medicine Man, who had spread before him a blanket on which lay many bunches of gay, colored yarn. In a basket was the rattle stick, a piece of straight cedar branch about twenty inches long, trimmed to perfect smoothness, with a tuft of foliage left at the top. The Medicine Man examined it critically, gave it a little extra final smoothing, made mysterious marks with his knife, and then began the

Little Medicine Man, 1932

trimming from a collection of objects before him. I could not verify them all and Timothy disclaims accurate knowledge, but I recognized eagle feathers, weeds and several little polished deer hoofs amongst them. These things were in turn firmly fixed with string near the top and the lengths of yarn were knotted down the length of the stick, so that when completed and entrusted to a man on horseback who was to carry it to another Medicine Man waiting in a hogan some miles away, it trailed in the breeze, its bright length seeming to beckon the mounted men who awaited its start, to follow.

I am told that the rattle stick is received in a ceremony in the distant hogan and is that night entrusted to a young girl who is responsible for its care during the days and nights which follow until the "sing" is over. The first night dance takes place at this hogan, the second at a place midway between the two, and the ceremony culminates on the third night at the patient's hogan where it was begun.

On the last day I went over to see the killing of the scalp. It had been buried some distance east of the hogan, the place being marked with a stake. Only men were admitted to Jim's hogan, where I could hear the Medicine Man's song and the sound of rattles going on, so I sat outside under a brush shelter and watched a rite which was coincidentally performed over Mrs. Jim by the daughter of the Medicine Man. Beneath a blanket her clothing was removed and her body painted with black paint, her clothing was replaced and her form was further draped with trailing lengths of colored cloth and new buckskin. Her face was also painted with the black paint and her hair, freshly washed, hung its black and shining length below her waist. From time to time small bowls of medicine were passed out from the hogan, given first to her to drink from and then offered to the women gathered for the ceremony.

Finally an old man was led from the hogan to the stake which marked the spot where the scalp was buried and there left to beat it with a stick, while Jim, with his body painted black, emerged and preceded his wife to a place where they together watched the old man's efforts.

After that, attention seemed turned to food and I found it time to take my leave, though I regretted that it was impossible for me to return that night for the dance and fun which ended the ceremony.

Colorado Springs
May 5, 1933

Dear Marion:

Your letter with its prospective visit promised reached me just as I was leaving Red Rock, and I am afraid your regret and disappointment at the news this letter bears will almost equal my own.

I have left Red Rock. I think I wrote you some time ago that due to the depression the finances of the Association employing me seemed very uncertain, and I have felt that as the latest addition to the staff it was perhaps up to me to step out and relieve the extra strain occasioned by my salary. This was hard to do, of course, for many reasons, particularly as the prospect of securing other work just now is doubtful, but another factor offered to strengthen my conviction. My dispensary was needed as dining room for the new school, and no other space was available. It is obviously impossible to work without quarters. I have, therefore, asked for leave of absence, which the Association has granted with the proviso that I return to its employ when things pick up.

Laura came down to help me pack and get off. I had carefully kept the news of my departure from all but my most intimate friends, knowing that I would be deluged and my packing hampered by visits. As it was, I found the move hard enough. The last morning brought those who did know to my porch before I was up, and breakfast had to stretch to feed the crowd. When the final farewells were said I saw Mrs. Francis' weeping head descend to Laura's shoulder, while the Ute Woman's less clean one sought mine. Timothy, not far from tears himself, interpreted her smothered wail for me: "She says, 'When I am hungry now I will have no place to eat!'" and I was ready to unpack!

My heart is truly hurt by the parting. They have become my friends, these people, and their affection and dependence have bound me with ties which are stronger than you might believe. Life amongst them has been far from easy in many ways, but the interest, sympathy, and wish to understand which they have inspired have made the hardship of little account. I only wish I might have formed a clearer picture of their needs—a more definite idea of how their future should be furthered. It is so difficult to forget one's own inherited and trained ideals and adapt to a much simpler and more primitive need. Of this I am sure, they are many years from ready to accept the complicated standards to which an accustomed civilization has adapted us. Are we not prone to over-estimate

Shepherds of the Desert, 1934

the value of these standards and overlook the value of their own, which, I am convinced, we are far from understanding?

It is distressing to see their partly educated youth returned to their home entirely out of tune and sympathy with the only life which circumstance offers. If this continues, what can the future hold for the race? It is a keen interest in their development which makes me loath to leave them. My small contribution to their comfort does not really matter. Individuals are born, suffer and die and the life of a race is not much affected by the alleviation of suffering in a few or the saving of a few lives. It is education which vitally affects the future, and one wishes it might be more intelligently directed.